W9-BOM-470

ORLAND PARK PUBLIC LIBRARY
14921 Ravinia Avenue
Orland Park, Illinois 60462
708-428-5100

DISCARD
MAY 2015

Energy Alternatives

Other Books of Related Interest:

Opposing Viewpoints Series
Endangered Oceans
The Environment
Natural Gas

At Issue Series
Biofuels
Fracking
Hybrid and Electric Cars
Wind Farms

Current Controversies Series
Gasoline
Global Warming
Oil Spills

"Congress shall make no law . . . abridging the freedom of speech, or of the press."

First Amendment to the US Constitution

The basic foundation of our democracy is the First Amendment guarantee of freedom of expression. The Opposing Viewpoints series is dedicated to the concept of this basic freedom and the idea that it is more important to practice it than to enshrine it.

OPPOSING
VIEWPOINTS®
SERIES

Energy Alternatives

Sylvia Engdahl, Book Editor

GREENHAVEN PRESS
A part of Gale, Cengage Learning

GALE
CENGAGE Learning·

Farmington Hills, Mich • San Francisco • New York • Waterville, Maine
Meriden, Conn • Mason, Ohio • Chicago

ORLAND PARK PUBLIC LIBRARY

Patricia Coryell, *Vice President & Publisher, New Products & GVRL*
Douglas Dentino, *Manager, New Products*
Judy Galens, *Acquisitions Editor*

© 2015 Greenhaven Press, a part of Gale, Cengage Learning.

WCN: 01-100-101

Gale and Greenhaven Press are registered trademarks used herein under license.

For more information, contact:
Greenhaven Press
27500 Drake Rd.
Farmington Hills, MI 48331-3535
Or you can visit our Internet site at gale.cengage.com

ALL RIGHTS RESERVED.
No part of this work covered by the copyright herein may be reproduced, transmitted, stored, or used in any form or by any means graphic, electronic, or mechanical, including but not limited to photocopying, recording, scanning, digitizing, taping, Web distribution, information networks, or information storage and retrieval systems, except as permitted under Section 107 or 108 of the 1976 United States Copyright Act, without the prior written permission of the publisher.

For product information and technology assistance, contact us at

Gale Customer Support, 1-800-877-4253
For permission to use material from this text or product, submit all requests online at www.cengage.com/permissions

Further permissions questions can be emailed to permissionrequest@cengage.com

Articles in Greenhaven Press anthologies are often edited for length to meet page requirements. In addition, original titles of these works are changed to clearly present the main thesis and to explicitly indicate the author's opinion. Every effort is made to ensure that Greenhaven Press accurately reflects the original intent of the authors. Every effort has been made to trace the owners of copyrighted material.

Cover Image copyright © Federico Rostagno/Shutterstock.com.

LIBRARY OF CONGRESS CATALOGING-IN-PUBLICATION DATA

Energy alternatives / Sylvia Engdahl, book editor.
  pages cm. -- (Opposing viewpoints)
  Includes bibliographical references and index.
  ISBN 978-0-7377-7258-6 (hardcover) -- ISBN 978-0-7377-7259-3 (pbk.)
  1. Renewable energy sources. I. Engdahl, Sylvia, editor.
  TJ808.E566 2015
  333.79'4--dc23
                                                        2014036031

Printed in the United States of America
1 2 3 4 5 6 7 19 18 17 16 15

Contents

Chapter 3: Is Utility-Scale Solar Power a Practical Alternative Energy Source?

Chapter 4: What Are the Advantages and Disadvantages of Other Energy Sources?

Why Consider Opposing Viewpoints?

"The only way in which a human being can make some approach to knowing the whole of a subject is by hearing what can be said about it by persons of every variety of opinion and studying all modes in which it can be looked at by every character of mind. No wise man ever acquired his wisdom in any mode but this."

John Stuart Mill

In our media-intensive culture it is not difficult to find differing opinions. Thousands of newspapers and magazines and dozens of radio and television talk shows resound with differing points of view. The difficulty lies in deciding which opinion to agree with and which "experts" seem the most credible. The more inundated we become with differing opinions and claims, the more essential it is to hone critical reading and thinking skills to evaluate these ideas. Opposing Viewpoints books address this problem directly by presenting stimulating debates that can be used to enhance and teach these skills. The varied opinions contained in each book examine many different aspects of a single issue. While examining these conveniently edited opposing views, readers can develop critical thinking skills such as the ability to compare and contrast authors' credibility, facts, argumentation styles, use of persuasive techniques, and other stylistic tools. In short, the Opposing Viewpoints Series is an ideal way to attain the higher-level thinking and reading skills so essential in a culture of diverse and contradictory opinions.

In addition to providing a tool for critical thinking, Opposing Viewpoints books challenge readers to question their own strongly held opinions and assumptions. Most people form their opinions on the basis of upbringing, peer pressure, and personal, cultural, or professional bias. By reading carefully balanced opposing views, readers must directly confront new ideas as well as the opinions of those with whom they disagree. This is not to argue simplistically that everyone who reads opposing views will—or should—change his or her opinion. Instead, the series enhances readers' understanding of their own views by encouraging confrontation with opposing ideas. Careful examination of others' views can lead to the readers' understanding of the logical inconsistencies in their own opinions, perspective on why they hold an opinion, and the consideration of the possibility that their opinion requires further evaluation.

Evaluating Other Opinions

To ensure that this type of examination occurs, Opposing Viewpoints books present all types of opinions. Prominent spokespeople on different sides of each issue as well as well-known professionals from many disciplines challenge the reader. An additional goal of the series is to provide a forum for other, less known, or even unpopular viewpoints. The opinion of an ordinary person who has had to make the decision to cut off life support from a terminally ill relative, for example, may be just as valuable and provide just as much insight as a medical ethicist's professional opinion. The editors have two additional purposes in including these less known views. One, the editors encourage readers to respect others' opinions—even when not enhanced by professional credibility. It is only by reading or listening to and objectively evaluating others' ideas that one can determine whether they are worthy of consideration. Two, the inclusion of such viewpoints encourages the important critical thinking skill of objectively evaluating an author's credentials and bias. This evaluation will illuminate an author's reasons for taking a particular stance on an issue and will aid in readers' evaluation of the author's ideas.

It is our hope that these books will give readers a deeper understanding of the issues debated and an appreciation of the complexity of even seemingly simple issues when good and honest people disagree. This awareness is particularly important in a democratic society such as ours in which people enter into public debate to determine the common good. Those with whom one disagrees should not be regarded as enemies but rather as people whose views deserve careful examination and may shed light on one's own.

Thomas Jefferson once said that "difference of opinion leads to inquiry, and inquiry to truth." Jefferson, a broadly educated man, argued that "if a nation expects to be ignorant and free . . . it expects what never was and never will be." As individuals and as a nation, it is imperative that we consider the opinions of others and examine them with skill and discernment. The Opposing Viewpoints series is intended to help readers achieve this goal.

David L. Bender and Bruno Leone,
Founders

Introduction

"We are like tenant farmers chopping
down the fence around our house for
fuel when we should be using Nature's
inexhaustible sources of energy—sun,
wind and tide."

—Thomas Edison in
conversation with Henry Ford and
Harvey Firestone (1931), as quoted
in Uncommon Friends: Life with
Thomas Edison, Henry Ford,
Harvey Firestone, Alexis Carrel and
Charles Lindbergh by James Newton

In recent years, increasing attention has been focused on alternative energy sources—that is, sources other than the fossil fuels oil, coal, and natural gas. Unlike fossil fuels, the alternatives are clean in the sense that they do not pollute the atmosphere, and most are renewable, meaning they are natural sources, such as sun and wind, that can never be depleted.

Currently, the most widely discussed reason for switching to alternative sources of energy is the belief that reducing the use of fossil fuels will stop or slow climate change. The majority of scientists are convinced that carbon dioxide emissions from the burning of fossil fuels are causing this change. "Emissions of carbon dioxide from the burning of fossil fuels have ushered in a new epoch where human activities will largely determine the evolution of Earth's climate," states a 2014 report from the Environmental Protection Agency (EPA). "Emission reductions choices made today matter in determining impacts experienced not just over the next few decades, but in the coming centuries and millennia."

Although this is the predominant theory and is often stated as fact, some scientists disagree. "There is no scientific proof that human emissions of carbon dioxide (CO_2) are the dominant cause of the minor warming of the earth's atmosphere over the past 100 years," ecologist Patrick Moore told a US Senate committee in February 2014. "What we do know with 'extreme certainty' is that the climate is always changing . . . and that we are not capable, with our limited knowledge, of predicting which way it will go next." Even if climate change is caused by human activity, eliminating the use of fossil fuels will not necessarily prevent further change. However, most people agree that it is wise to be on the safe side and limit carbon emissions.

Moreover, there are other benefits to be gained by minimizing the use of fossil fuels. Pollution in the atmosphere caused by fossil fuel use is harmful to health. The EPA estimates that reducing carbon emissions from power plants alone by 30 percent will, by 2030, avoid 2,700 to 6,600 premature deaths per year and 140,000 to 150,000 asthma attacks in children.

Renewable energy sources will surely have to be utilized someday, since Earth's supply of fossil fuels will eventually run out. Estimates as to how long these fuels will last vary widely, but sooner or later they will be exhausted. It will then be too late to turn to other energy sources that have not already been developed, for solving the technological problems and making the transition will be a long process. For this reason, if for no other, humankind must start in advance to use renewable sources that will always be available.

It has generally been assumed that alternative energy sources are friendly to the environment. Recently, however, it has become apparent that no source of energy is entirely free of adverse environmental impact, and more and more concerns are being raised about those originally thought harmless. Damming rivers for hydroelectric power, a well-established renewable source of energy, has long been known to destroy wildlife habitats and harm fish, and for this reason it has lost favor. Newer energy sources also cause damage. Wind farms endanger birds, and if offshore, disrupt marine life; the extent to which they affect human health is uncertain. While a few wind turbines may not spoil the landscape, some people are beginning to worry about what it would be like to have forests of them all over the planet. Utility-scale solar power plants are also damaging to wildlife; while a few in isolated areas may do no harm, large numbers of vast land-covering installations, some types of which produce solar flux hot enough to melt the feathers off birds flying by, might be less tolerable. Biomass power is favorable when waste materials are used for fuel, but growing crops specifically for power generation—and worse, cutting down forests—has been found to result in more carbon dioxide pollution than fossil fuels. Additionally, hydraulic fracturing, or fracking, of the ground to release natural gas or geothermal power can contaminate groundwater and cause earthquakes.

Nuclear power is a special case. It is a clean alternative to fossil fuels, and even some environmentalists are coming to favor it for this reason, along with many other individuals who believe it should not be abandoned. However, should a serious accident occur, a nuclear power plant can produce radiation that kills thousands and makes the land uninhabitable for generations. Experts are divided as to whether adequate power plant design can achieve full protection against accidents; the public fears it cannot.

It appears that there is no such thing as a completely safe source of power. This is not surprising; since humans first discovered fire, it has been known that power is by its nature both essential to civilization and potentially harmful. Throughout history, it has been necessary to balance benefits with risks. Today, more is known about risks that were formerly ignored, and risks not only to humans but also to wildlife are considered; but the principle remains the same. Humankind needs energy; the only question is how to harness it with as little detrimental effect as possible at a cost people can afford. Most experts agree that there is no single "best" way and that a mixture of power sources should be utilized.

Opposing Viewpoints: Energy Alternatives examines some of the pros and cons of various alternative energy sources in chapters titled "Can Alternative Energy Sources Effectively Replace Fossil Fuels?," "Do the Benefits of Wind Power Outweigh Its Disadvantages?," "Is Utility-Scale Solar Power a Practical Alternative Energy Source?," and "What Are the Advantages and Disadvantages of Other Energy Sources?" The authors of the viewpoints discuss the possibilities of alternative energy sources that may power the world as the earth's fossil fuels will someday reach depletion.

CHAPTER 1

Can Alternative Energy Sources Effectively Replace Fossil Fuels?

Chapter Preface

On June 2, 2014, US president Barack Obama's administration announced the first national regulations requiring power plants to limit carbon emissions, which in the opinion of most—but not all—scientists are a cause of Earth's continuing climate change.

The proposed regulations, which were issued by the Environmental Protection Agency (EPA) under the president's executive authority and do not require congressional action, are extremely controversial. They are expected to have major political repercussions and may face legal challenges. There will be a period of public comment before the details are finalized, but the goal is to force states to reduce carbon emissions by 30 percent from 2005 levels by 2030. According to the EPA, this is equal to the emissions from powering more than half the homes in the United States for one year.

Many environmental and state leaders greeted the announcement with approval. "I applaud EPA's new carbon rules, which will unleash clean energy innovation and reduce energy costs while protecting our environment and public health," said Governor Deval Patrick of Massachusetts. "This is a critical step in moving the nation toward a clean energy future."

However, many others disapprove. The strongest protests come from those concerned about the closure of coal mines. Coal is the source of the largest percentage of America's energy, yet it produces the highest level of carbon emissions. Thousands of workers depend on coal mining for their livelihood. Also, some experts fear that if other sources of energy are not fully developed by the time the deadline arrives, the nation may face an energy shortage, and it will then be too late to reestablish the coal industry. "The administration has set out to kill coal and its 800,000 jobs," said Senator Michael B. Enzi of Wyoming, according to the *New York Times*. "If it succeeds in death by regulation, we'll all be paying a lot more money for electricity—if we can get it. Our pocketbook will be lighter, but our country will be darker."

Senator Mitch McConnell of Kentucky voiced similar objections: "The impact on individuals and families and entire regions of the country will be catastrophic, as a proud domestic industry is decimated—and many of its jobs shipped overseas. . . . The downstream effects of today's announcement will be staggering for millions."

Peabody Energy, the world's largest private sector coal company, declared, "American policy should be guided not by a modeled crisis, but by the real crisis of more than one of every three US households that qualify for energy assistance. Energy inequality in the United States is an enormous challenge . . . and access to low-cost energy is a basic need."

Although the use of coal will decline under the new rule, the EPA estimates that it will still provide more than 30 percent of the nation's power, and observers have pointed out that its dominance is already threatened by increasing use of natural gas. Moreover, not all states depend on coal; natural gas or hydroelectric power dominates in some, and development of renewable energy sources is under way everywhere.

The impact of the EPA regulations will vary from state to state and may not increase energy costs everywhere. One thing is certain: Efforts to develop new ways of generating power will be stimulated. The viewpoints in this chapter discuss whether alternative energy sources can effectively replace fossil fuels.

"A massive public-private partnership is needed in the United States to develop smart-grid, distributed generation technology."

Society Needs Decentralized and Renewable Energy Alternatives

Steven Cohen

In the following viewpoint, Steven Cohen argues that all nations are dependent on an energy infrastructure that is vulnerable and that climate change is a sign that transitioning from risky sources of power to renewable ones is necessary. The main problems, he says, lie in achieving this while consumption of energy is growing throughout the world and in convincing companies that are heavily invested in the present system to invest in renewable energy instead. Also, he states, the ultimate goal is for individual homes and businesses to be able to generate and store their own electric power. Cohen is the executive director of Columbia University's Earth Institute.

Steven Cohen, "We Need Decentralized and Renewable Energy," *Huffington Post*, November 7, 2011. Copyright © 2011 by Steven Cohen. All rights reserved. Reproduced by permission.

As you read, consider the following questions:

1. According to Cohen, what is the cause of large-scale power outages in winter?

2. According to Cohen, why is reducing consumption not the answer to the energy crisis?

3. What precedent does Cohen see for using the tax laws to encourage people to generate their own energy from renewable sources?

The surprise snow storm that hit the Northeast of the United States at the end of October [2011] resulted in massive power outages and reminded us of our dependency on energy. Without plentiful, easily accessible energy we must do without heat, cooling, refrigeration and light. We also lose television, the Internet and the ability to recharge our smartphones. While we can get a lot more efficient in our use of energy, our dependence on energy and use of electronic technology continues to grow. And not just here in the United States. As nations such as India and China grow their economies, they increase their use of energy as well. Unfortunately, as we discovered here after the recent storm, we are dependent on a centralized massive energy infrastructure, one that is more vulnerable to disruption than we would like to think.

Let's focus on the issue of centralized, capital-intensive production facilities. With the growth of the 21st century's globally interconnected economy, we find that large multinational corporations are developing differently than companies did in the 20th century. They are less identified with their nation of origin, and often rely on a large number of smaller companies to provide them with essential elements of their production process. These smaller suppliers are located all over the world. This "networked" style of management has been made possible by a number of key technologies: low-cost computing, the Internet, smartphones, satellite communication, containerized shipping and bar codes. These complex production networks are still vulnerable to disruption, such as the supply shortages faced by the auto industry after this year's massive earthquake in Japan. However, they are far more resilient than the highly centralized, capital-intensive energy system we all depend on. In a global supply chain, if one supplier is unavailable, others often can be found. Electricity doesn't work that way. If your utility stops sending you power, there is no store across the street you can switch to.

In the case of the recent energy outages in the Northeast, the problem was not with the generation of energy, but with its distribution. The weather knocked out power lines and other transmission equipment. Power generators were not disrupted. In summer heat waves, however, most of the problem stems from inadequate generation of power.

In the 2011 version of the energy crisis, we face problems with both power generation and distribution. In some places, during certain times of the year, energy use puts a strain on energy generation facilities. In addition, energy generation poses risks to human health and ecological systems first when we extract fossil fuels from the earth, and again when we burn the fuel. Seeing this danger, some environmentalists have taken another look at nuclear power. Then came the nuclear disaster in Japan, which reminded us of the risks of nuclear power. The probability of risk is low, but once incurred, the intensity of risk is quite high. The Gulf oil spill [referring to the Deepwater Horizon oil spill of 2010 in the Gulf of Mexico near Mississippi], mountaintop removal for coal, and hydrofracking for natural gas are vivid examples of the environmental impact of extracting fossil fuels from the crust of the earth.

Renewable Energy Is Essential

The very real dangers of climate change are a warning that we need to begin the transition from fossil fuels to renewable energy. The trick is doing this while the worldwide consumption

Cost-Effective Energy Sources Must Be Found

When they decide between the immediacy of a household budget and an uncertain energy and ecological future, most people frankly do not understand and cannot afford to care about the long-term impacts of their decisions. Globally, most people lack the necessary information or day-to-day economic security that would allow them to understand and act on the long-term effects of small, daily choices. Their priorities are feeding themselves and their families, staying warm and safe, and carving out whatever security they can. To meet their vital needs, people and the societies they [make up] will continue to absorb trees, fossil fuels, and food stocks unless and until accessible and cost-effective energy choices exist. The history of our species . . . is a repetition of this story. It is the story of a species trying to improve its lot and, through ingenuity or chance, tapping into a new source of food or energy. This species eats and multiplies until the available food and energy are dwarfed by the population, followed by a painful adjustment in lives and economic livelihood until a new equilibrium is found.

Travis Bradford, Solar Revolution:
The Economic Transformation of the Global Energy Industry.
Cambridge, MA: MIT Press, 2006.

of energy continues to grow at a ferocious pace. The other trick is to convince companies that have billions of dollars in sunk costs in the current energy system to stop lobbying against renewable energy and start investing in it.

It is silly to think that anything short of economic or natural catastrophe can stop increased energy use across the globe. People tell me all the time that the answer to this energy and sustainability crisis is to reduce consumption. I see no signs of that happening. It is possible to shift individual consumption to less resource-consumptive and less environmentally damaging behaviors, but an overall reduction in economic consumption is not going to happen in the United States and is certainly not going to happen in Asia and Africa. . . .

So what do we do? Is there a solution to this crisis of sustainability? I think there is. The heart of the issue is energy. We need to decentralize production and increase the resiliency of the energy distribution system. A massive public-private partnership is needed in the United States to develop smart-grid, distributed generation technology. We also need to work on the development of decentralized, small-scale energy generation. Ultimately, each home and business should be capable of generating, storing and sharing energy. Solar, wind, geothermal, and perhaps some other technology yet to be invented must be subsidized to make them cheaper than fossil fuels. At some point, the subsidies will no longer be needed.

Communities, households and businesses must be encouraged via the tax code to become energy generators. There is of course a precedent for such a massive government intervention in the private market place. It is called home ownership. In 1940, 43.6% of all American households owned their own homes. By 1960 that had reached 61.9%. This was made possible by making mortgage interest tax deductible and by government-backed mortgage insurance. Yes, I know that during the past two decades we made huge mistakes in housing finance and policy that led to the massive foreclosures of the last several years. That still does not mean that the basic policy of facilitating home ownership was a mistake. We need similar policy creativity to increase the percentage of people generating energy from renewable sources.

As the rest of the economy moves away from capital-intensive, highly centralized production facilities, we need to do the same with energy. As we take that step, let's also replace our dependence on fossil fuels with renewable forms of energy. Let's increase government spending on the basic science and R&D [research and development] needed to develop the breakthrough technologies needed for the transition off of fossil fuels.

| "Whether what propels a car is electricity, liquid fuels, natural gas, or hydrogen, the critical impacts all occur far from the car itself at locations where fuels originate and natural resources are exploited."

Promoting Alternative Fuels for Vehicles Is a Waste of Taxpayers' Money

John DeCicco

In the following viewpoint, John DeCicco argues that it is pointless and a waste of tax money to push alternative fuels for vehicles because use of petroleum-based fuel has little if any environmental impact compared to the use of fossil fuels presently required to produce such alternatives. The emphasis, he says, should be on controlling carbon emissions from power plants rather than on encouraging electric vehicles. In his opinion, no alternative fuel will be of any benefit until it can be produced without damage to the environment, and by that time today's fuel technologies may be obsolete. DeCicco is a researcher at the University of Michigan's Energy Institute and a professor in the university's School of Natural Resources and Environment.

John DeCicco, "Why Pushing Alternate Fuels Makes for Bad Public Policy," *Environment 360*, August 22, 2013. Copyright © 2013 by John DeCicco. All rights reserved. Reproduced by permission.

As you read, consider the following questions:

1. In DeCicco's opinion, what three actions would be preferable to promoting the use of alternative fuels for cars?

2. According to DeCicco, why does the use of biofuels for cars not make sense?

3. Why is fueling vehicles with natural gas of little or no benefit to the environment, according to the viewpoint?

For nearly four decades, every American president has promoted alternative fuel vehicles as a way to secure the country's energy independence. Ronald Reagan backed the 1988 Alternative Motor Fuels Act, which championed development of nonpetroleum fuels. George H.W. Bush helped shape the 1992 Energy Policy Act, whose goal was to displace 30 percent of U.S. transportation oil use by 2010. Bill Clinton ramped up those initiatives, launching the Clean Cities program to promote alternative fuels. George W. Bush gave particular support to hydrogen fuel cell vehicles and worked with Congress to create the Renewable Fuel Standard, which mandates a large increase in biofuel use that has now reached 16 billion gallons a year, mainly ethanol.

And President [Barack] Obama—under the misguided presumption that alternative fuels emit significantly fewer greenhouse gases than gasoline, and goaded by green groups and alternative fuel business interests—has been a staunch proponent of alternative fuels and electric vehicles (EVs). The president's first-term economic stimulus allocated an additional $300 million for alternative fuel vehicle deployment. His administration has enthusiastically promoted EVs, pledging to put a million electric vehicles on the road by 2015. Obama's new climate plan, unveiled in June [2013], calls for ongoing efforts to deploy biofuels, EVs, and hydrogen fuel cell cars.

Despite this bipartisan support stretching back almost 40 years, the fact is that using government mandates and subsidies to promote politically favored fuels *du jour* is a waste of taxpayers' money. It's also a diversion from what really needs to be done to reduce transportation-related greenhouse gas emissions. Examining alternative fuels as they are produced today, as opposed to how some people wish they'll be produced in a hoped-for renewable energy future, reveals no environmentally persuasive reason to rush alternative fuel vehicles onto the road.

To be sure, fundamental science and engineering research are important for creating new options for the future, and so a well-hedged set of alternative fuel vehicle options has a place in the federal research and development portfolio. But as for going beyond laboratory research and development, a rigorous analysis shows that subsidizing deployment of alternative fuels and vehicles—totaling billions of dollars over the last 40 years—is a misplaced priority. The Renewable Fuel Standard, the $7,500 tax credit for electric cars, the alternative fuel promotions of the Clean Cities program—these and decades of other programs—go well beyond research and development by trying to push alternative fuels and vehicles into the marketplace.

Instead, in order to reduce transportation-related greenhouse gas emissions, action is needed on three fronts: continuing to raise fuel efficiency standards, pursuing policies to reduce driving, and, most importantly, controlling carbon *upstream* in the energy and resource systems that supply the fuels used *downstream* in our everyday lives.

Electric Vehicles

In the case of electric vehicles, an upstream focus means cutting CO_2 emissions from power plants, as Obama has proposed in his new climate plan. Without low-carbon power generation, EVs will have little lasting value. Similarly, for biofuels such as ethanol, any potential climate benefit is entirely upstream on land where feedstocks are grown. Biofuels have no benefit downstream, where used as motor fuels, because their tailpipe CO_2 emissions differ only trivially from those of gasoline.

Given how difficult the climate policy debate has been, it's crucial to prioritize where our money, time, and attention are focused. Even if certain alternative fuel vehicle technologies (say EVs) may play an important role in the decades ahead, these technologies are unlikely to take the form being prematurely subsidized today. What's at issue is not just the waste of tax dollars, but the squandering of public goodwill due to the hyping of alternatives.

Whether what propels a car is electricity, liquid fuels, natural gas, or hydrogen, the critical impacts all occur far from the car itself at locations where fuels originate and natural resources are exploited. Today, none of the relevant sectors—electric power generation, oil and gas supply, agriculture and land—are close to having their carbon impacts adequately managed.

Take electricity, for example. In the United States, most of it still comes from fossil fuels—37 percent coal and 30 percent natural gas, as of last year. Recent shifts to natural gas have had only a modest effect; CO_2 from electricity generation is declining, but slowly, at a projected rate of less than one percent per year. But thanks to stronger fuel economy standards pushed by the Obama administration, the CO_2 emissions rate of U.S. automobiles is on track to decline by 2.1 percent a year, more than double the rate of reduction in the power sector.

Given the gains in gasoline vehicle efficiency, the climate benefits of electric vehicles will shrink unless more is done to reduce emissions when generating electricity. Because power plants are retired much more slowly than cars are scrapped, government spending to rush EVs onto the road and underwrite their infrastructure is not money well spent. By the time the power sector is clean enough and battery costs fall enough for EVs to cut carbon at a significant scale, self-driving cars and wireless charging will probably render today's electric vehicle technologies obsolete. Accelerating power sector cleanup is far more important than plugging in the car fleet.

Biofuel Vehicles

As for ethanol and other biofuels, a National Academy of Sciences report concluded that their climate benefits are highly uncertain. The study found that the Renewable Fuel Standard—now at 16 billion gallons and climbing—may not reduce greenhouse gas emissions at all once global impacts are counted. A pioneer in fuel cycle studies—Mark A. Delucchi of the University of California, Davis, Institute of Transportation Studies—now questions the accuracy of any of the greenhouse gas analyses used to promote biofuels.

In fact, biofuels have no climate benefit on the road, which is where they are burned. If there is a benefit, it happens on land and occurs only if harvesting biofuel feedstocks causes a net additional removal of carbon dioxide from the air. Take corn, which is the main feedstock for making ethanol. Growing the corn that becomes ethanol absorbs no more carbon from the air than the corn that goes into cattle feed or cornflakes. Burning the ethanol releases essentially the same amount of CO_2 as burning gasoline. No less CO_2 went into the air from the tailpipe; no more CO_2 was removed from the air at the cornfield. So where's the climate benefit?

Until that question can be carefully answered for fuel produced on a large, commercial scale—as opposed to limited and costly experimental methods—it is not possible to scientifically determine the extent to which biofuels actually benefit the climate. The implication? We need to ensure that biomass feedstocks really do absorb more CO_2 than whatever else might be growing on the land. For now, it makes more sense

Biofuels Harm the Environment

Once viewed as the Holy Grail of environmental protection, renewables increasingly are coming under fire for their large ecological footprint. Biofuels particularly have been the subject of numerous peer-reviewed studies showing the harmful effects of using corn, soybeans, and even switchgrass as a source for transportation fuel. . . .

A 2007 study in *Science* magazine by scientists with the Nature Conservancy and the University of Minnesota caused a flood of debate after reporting that clearing rain forests, savannas, and grasslands to produce biofuels in Brazil, Asia, and the U.S. could release up to 420 times more carbon dioxide than fossil fuels.

Other studies, including the international Organisation for Economic Co-operation and Development's (OECD), reported: "When . . . soil acidification, fertilizer use, biodiversity loss, and toxicity of agricultural pesticides are taken into account, the overall environmental impacts of ethanol and biofuels can very easily exceed those of petrol and mineral diesel." . . .

Similarly, a study by the World Wildlife Fund concludes, "Biofuels are a bad deal for forests, wildlife and the climate if they replace tropical rain forests. In fact, they hasten climate change by removing one of the world's most efficient carbon storage tools—intact tropical rain forests."

Dana Joel Gattuso,
"Renewable Energy: Truth and Consequences,"
National Center for Public Policy Research, September 2009.

to soak up CO_2 through reforestation and redouble efforts to protect forests rather than producing biofuels, which puts carbon-rich natural lands at risk.

As for hydrogen fuel cell cars, the benefits depend on low greenhouse gas hydrogen production. Today, hydrogen is produced from natural gas or during petroleum refining, and commercially available hydrogen involves about 35 percent more greenhouse gas emissions per unit of energy than gasoline. Hydrogen fuel cell cars are more efficient than today's gasoline cars, but their ultimate value depends on extensive changes upstream in the industrial sectors where hydrogen is generated.

Similarly, the climate benefits of natural gas vehicles depend on the control of upstream emissions, particularly methane. Because natural gas combustion emits only 22 percent less carbon dioxide than gasoline per unit of energy, and any methane leaks undermine that modest benefit, the climate benefits of natural gas vehicles are marginal at best.

Whatever fuel is considered, the real need is to limit the greenhouse gas emissions that now remain largely uncontrolled in the sectors from which fuels are sourced. This conclusion is based on a detailed analysis that works forward from present realities rather than backward from one imaginary future or another. Although one or more alternative fuels might have a role to play someday, which alternatives will be needed, and when, cannot be determined on the basis of current data. It's also quite possible that none will be relevant in the forms that alternative fuel vehicles are being promoted today. Moreover, given the poor track record of alternative fuels to date, there's no need to saddle climate policy with this legacy of disco-era, "anything but oil" energy policy.

> "The bottom line: We are going to run
> out of fossil fuels for energy, and we
> have no choice but to prepare for the
> new age of energy production."

Diverse Alternative Energy Sources Will Be Essential to the Future

Eric McLamb

In the following viewpoint, Eric McLamb points out that fossil fuels cannot last long enough to meet the world's energy needs, especially in view of population growth, and that only a small percentage of energy is now obtained from renewable sources. He states that the biggest problem with the use of fossil fuels is the damage they do to the environment, yet no single renewable energy source is sufficient in itself to replace fossil fuels. Therefore, he says, it is necessary to develop diverse energy technologies to meet energy needs. McLamb is the founder, chief executive officer, and president of the Ecology Communications Group Inc.

Eric McLamb, "Fossil Fuels vs. Renewable Energy Resources," Ecology.com, Ecology Today, September 6, 2011. Ecology.com is the central website for the Ecology Global Network, a service of Ecology Communications Group, Inc. This article also appears in the Energy section of Ecology.com. Copyright © Ecology Global Network. All rights reserved. Reproduced by permission.

As you read, consider the following questions:

1. How long ago did fossil fuels begin to form, according to the viewpoint?

2. According to McLamb, how much longer are fossil fuel reserves estimated to last?

3. What is the main reason solar power cannot be a major worldwide power source in the near future, according to McLamb?

There is a great deal of information and enthusiasm today about the development and increased production of our global energy needs from alternative energy sources. Solar energy, wind power and moving water are all traditional sources of alternative energy that are making progress. The enthusiasm everyone shares for these developments has in many ways created a sense of complacency that our future energy demands will easily be met.

Alternative energy is an interesting concept when you think about it. In our global society, it simply means energy that is produced from sources other than our primary energy supply: fossil fuels. Coal, oil and natural gas are the three kinds of fossil fuels that we have mostly depended on for our energy needs, from home heating and electricity to fuel for our automobiles and mass transportation.

The problem is fossil fuels are nonrenewable. They are limited in supply and will one day be depleted. There is no escaping this conclusion. Fossil fuels formed from plants and animals that lived hundreds of millions of years ago and became buried way underneath the earth's surface where their remains collectively transformed into the combustible materials we use for fuel.

In fact, the earliest known fossil fuel deposits are from the Cambrian period about 500 million years ago, way before the dinosaurs emerged onto the scene. This is when most of the major groups of animals first appeared on Earth. The later fossil fuels—which provide more substandard fuels like peat or lignite coal (soft coal)—began forming as late as five million years ago in the Pliocene period. At our rate of consumption, these fuels cannot occur fast enough to meet our current or future energy demands.

Despite the promise of alternative energy sources—more appropriately called renewable energy—collectively they provide only about 7 percent of the world's energy needs (Source: Energy Information Administration). This means that fossil fuels, along with nuclear energy—a controversial, nonrenewable energy source—are supplying 93 percent of the world's energy resources.

Nuclear energy, which is primarily generated by splitting atoms, only provides 6 percent of the world's energy supplies. Still, nuclear energy is not likely to be a major source of world energy consumption because of public pressure and the relative dangers associated with unleashing the power of the atom. Yet, governments such as the United States see its vast potential and are placing pressure on the further exploitation of nuclear energy.

The total world energy demand is for about 400 quadrillion British Thermal Units—or BTUs—each year (Source: US Department of Energy). That's 400,000,000,000,000,000 BTUs! A BTU is roughly equal to the energy and heat generated by a match. Oil, coal and natural gas supply nearly 88 percent of the world's energy needs, or about 350 quadrillion BTUs. Of this amount, oil is king, providing about 41 percent of the world's total energy supplies, or about 164 quadrillion BTU. Coal provides 24 percent of the world's energy, or 96 quadrillion BTUs, and natural gas provides the remaining 22 percent, or 88 quadrillion BTUs.

It's not so much that we mine fossil fuels for our consumption any more than it is to mine salt or tap water supplies way underground. The problems occur when we destroy ecosystems while mining it and while using it. Certainly, if there were a way that fossil fuels can be mined and used in ways that do not harm our ecology, then everything will be okay ... in a perfect world. What makes our world perfect is that it really isn't perfect according to definition. It is natural, with all things interdependent on each other to live, grow and produce. Fossil fuel mining and oil production can and have caused irreparable damage to our environment.

The Fossil Fuel Dilemma

Fossil fuels exist, and they provide a valuable service. It's not so much that we use fossil fuels for energy that is problematic, but it's the side effects of using them that cause all of the problems. Burning fossil fuels creates carbon dioxide, the number one greenhouse gas contributing to global warming. Combustion of these fossil fuels is considered to be the largest contributing factor to the release of greenhouse gases into the atmosphere. In the 20th century, the average temperature of Earth rose 1 degree Fahrenheit (1°F). This was a period that saw the most prolific population growth and industrial development (read use of energy) in Earth's history.

The impact of global warming on the environment is extensive and affects many areas. In the Arctic and Antarctica, warmer temperatures are causing the ice to melt, which will increase sea level and change the composition of the surrounding seawater. Rising sea levels alone can impede processes ranging from settlement, agriculture and fishing both commercially and recreationally. Air pollution is also a direct result of the use of fossil fuels, resulting in smog and the degradation of human health and plant growth.

But there's also the great dangers posed to natural ecosystems that result from collecting fossil fuels, particularly coal and oil. Oil spills have devastated ecosystems and coal mining has stripped lands of their vitality. This is the primary reason to discontinue the pursuit to tap the vast oil reserves in the Arctic National Wildlife Refuge (ANWR).

The oil, coal and natural gas companies know these are serious problems. But until our renewable energy sources become more viable as major energy providers, the only alternative for our global population is for these companies to continue tapping into the fossil fuel reserves to meet our energy needs. And you can pretty much count on these companies being there providing energy from renewable sources when the fossil fuels are depleted. Many oil companies, for example, are involved in the development of more reliable renewable energy technologies. For example, British Petroleum, today known as BP, has become one of the world's leading providers of solar energy through its BP Solar division, a business that they are planning on eclipsing their oil production business in the near future.

Future Supplies for Future Energy

Just how limited are our fossil fuel reserves? Some estimates say our fossil fuel reserves will be depleted within 50 years, while others say it will be 100–120 years. The fact is that neither one of these projections is very appealing for a global community that is so heavily dependent on fossil fuels to meet basic human needs. The bottom line: We are going to run out of fossil fuels for energy, and we have no choice but to prepare for the new age of energy production since, most certainly, human demands for energy will not decrease.

Nobody really knows when the last drop of oil, lump of coal or cubic foot of natural gas will be collected from the earth. All of it will depend on how well we manage our energy demands along with how well we can develop and use renewable energy sources.

And here is one very important factor: population growth. As the population grows upwards towards nine billion people over the next 50 years, the world's energy demands will in-

Renewable Energy Is the Only Solution

There is one forecast of which you can already be sure: Someday renewable energy will be the only way for people to satisfy their energy needs. Because of the physical, ecological and (therefore) social limits to nuclear and fossil energy use, ultimately nobody will be able to circumvent renewable energy as the solution, even if it turns out to be everybody's last remaining choice. The question keeping everyone in suspense, however, is whether we shall succeed in making this radical change of energy platforms happen early enough to spare the world irreversible ecological mutilation and political and economic catastrophe.

Hermann Scheer,
Energy Autonomy: The Economic, Social
and Technological Case for Renewable Energy.
New York: Routledge, 2006.

crease proportionately. Not only will it be important for renewable energy to keep up with the increasing population growth, but it must outpace not only these demands but begin replacing fossil fuel energy production if we are to meet future energy needs.

By the year 2020, world energy consumption is projected to increase by 50 percent, or an additional 207 quadrillion BTUs. If the global consumption of renewable energy sources remains constant, the world's available fossil fuel reserves will be consumed in 104 years or early in the 22nd century (Source: US Department of Energy). Clearly, renewable energy resources will play an increasingly vital role in the power-generation mix over the next century.

The Ultimate Energy Sources
as the Underdogs

Sun, wind and water are perfect energy sources . . . depending on where you are. They are nonpolluting, renewable and efficient. They are simple: All you need is sunlight, running water and/or wind. Not only does the use of renewable energy sources help reduce global carbon dioxide emissions, but it also adds some much-needed flexibility to the energy resource mix by decreasing our dependence on limited reserves of fossil fuels.

Essentially, these renewable energy sources create their own energy. The object is to capture and harness their mechanical power and convert it to electricity in the most effective and productive manner possible. There's more than enough renewable energy sources to supply all of the world's energy needs forever; however, the challenge is to develop the capability to effectively and economically capture, store and use the energy when needed.

Take solar energy for example. The ultimate source of energy is the sun. Its energy is found in all things, including fossil fuels. Plants depend on the sun to make food, animals eat the plants, and both ended up becoming the key ingredients for fossil fuels. Without the sun, nothing on this planet would exist.

The sun also provides enough energy that can be stored for use long after the sun sets and even during extended cloudy periods. But making it available is much easier said than done. It would be cost prohibitive to make solar energy mainstream for major world consumption in the near future. The technology is pretty much ready for many business and consumer applications, but it would be way too expensive to replace the current energy infrastructure used for fossil fuel energy. Still, according to the European Photovoltaic Industry Association, solar power could provide energy for more than one billion people by 2020 and 26 percent of global energy needs by 2040.

Wind and hydroelectric power, which have been used effectively for generations, are also rapidly growing energy markets. The principle behind both is that the force of the wind and water currents are passed through turbines, which convert their energy into electricity. Commercial wind energy is usually collected by wind "farms" essentially consisting of hundreds of wind turbines (windmills) spread over large plots of land.

But hydroelectric power is harnessed in several different methods. The most popular is through dams, such as the Hoover Dam on the Colorado River. Another form of hydroelectric energy is tidal power. In use since the early 1900s, tidal power stations collect the energy created by the rise and fall of the tides to convert to electricity.

Biomass energy, or energy from burning plants and other organic matter, is one of man's earliest sources of energy. Wood was once the main source of power for heat, and it still is in many developing countries. Most people in developed countries use wood only for aesthetic purposes or secondary heating, limited mainly to fireplaces and decorative woodstoves. Roughly one to two billion people in the developing nations still use wood as their primary source of heat. It is this group that is seen being among the first to convert to solar heating and energy because there is no other existing infrastructure to hinder its development.

Perhaps the best solution to our growing energy challenges comes from the Union of Concerned Scientists: "No single solution can meet our society's future energy needs. The solution instead will come from a family of diverse energy technologies that share a common thread—they do not deplete our natural resources or destroy our environment."

| "The energy that can be extracted from renewable sources, relative to that from conventional forms, by its very nature is limited and expensive."

Alternative Energy Sources Are Too Costly and Unreliable

Benjamin Zycher

In the following viewpoint, Benjamin Zycher explains why he believes the government should not subsidize renewable energy development. He says advocates have overlooked a number of factors that conclude that producing power from renewable sources will never be economical: Wind and solar power plants require far more land and equipment than power from conventional sources; the places where they can be located are limited; and because they are unreliable, they require backup sources of power. Zycher is a resident scholar at the American Enterprise Institute for Public Policy Research (AEI), where he works on energy and environmental policy. He is also a senior fellow at the Pacific Research Institute.

Benjamin Zycher, "Renewable Energy Subsidies Should Be Abandoned," Statement before the Senate Finance Committee, March 27, 2012.

As you read, consider the following questions:

1. According to Zycher, why does the nature of wind and solar energy make it inherently more expensive to harness than fossil fuel energy?

2. Why will the transmission cost of wind and solar power always be higher for the nation as a whole than the cost of transmitting conventional power, according to Zycher?

3. According to the viewpoint, why have state requirements for using wind power, when it is available, sometimes made air pollution worse?

The implementation of energy policies in the U.S. for decades has pursued energy sources defined in various ways as alternative, unconventional, independent, renewable, and clean, in an effort to replace such conventional fuels as oil, coal, and natural gas. These long-standing efforts without exception have yielded poor outcomes, in a nutshell because they must swim against the tide of market forces. That is why the only reliable outcome has been one disappointment after another, and there are powerful reasons to predict that the same will prove true with respect to the current enthusiasm for renewable electricity.

Policy preferences for renewable electricity at both the federal and state levels are substantial, in the form of both direct and indirect financial subsidies, and other forms of support as well. The relative magnitudes of the federal subsidies given various forms of electricity, as estimated by the Energy Information Administration [EIA], are instructive. For 2010, non-hydroelectric renewable power generation, again, was 3.6 percent of all generation; but it received 53.5 percent of all federal financial support for the electric power sector. Wind power, providing 2.3 percent of generation, received 42 percent of such support. This combination of substantial policy support and meager market competitiveness suggests the presence of important impediments to the growth of renewable power. The technical literature reveals three central problems that have not received widespread attention in the popular discussion; they can be denoted as:

- The unconcentrated energy content of renewable energy sources.

- Location (or siting)—that is, geographic—limitations and resulting transmission costs.

- Relatively low availability ("capacity factors") over time combined with the intermittent nature of wind flows and sunlight.

Unconcentrated Energy Content

The energy content of wind flows and sunlight, which varies depending upon air speed and sunlight intensity, is far less concentrated than that of the energy contained in fossil or nuclear fuels. In order to compensate for this physical characteristic, large capital investments in land and/or materials must be made to make renewable generation even technically practical in terms of generating nontrivial amounts of electricity. A wind farm would require 500 wind turbines of 2 MW [megawatt] each to provide a theoretical generation capacity of 1000 MW. Since the wind turbines must be spaced apart to avoid wake effects (wind interference among the turbines), a 1000 MW wind farm even in principle would require on the order of 48,000–64,000 acres (or 75–100 square miles) of land. With an assumed capacity factor for a typical wind farm of, say, 35 percent, reliable wind capacity of 1000 MW would require an amount of land (perhaps at different locations) on the order of two to three times that rough estimate. In contrast, a 1000 MW gas-fired plant requires about 10–15 acres; conventional coal, natural gas, and nuclear plants have capacity factors of 85–90 percent.

The same general problem afflicts solar power. The energy content of sunlight, crudely, is about 150–400 watts per square meter, depending on location, of which about 20–30 percent is convertible to electricity, depending on the particular technology. Accordingly, even in theory a square meter of solar energy receiving capacity is enough to power roughly one 100-watt lightbulb, putting aside such issues of sunlight intensity and the like. This problem of land requirements for solar thermal facilities is of sufficient importance that most analyses assume a maximum plant capacity of 50–100 MW, which, conservatively, would require approximately 1250 acres, or 2 square miles.

In short: Transformation of the unconcentrated energy content of wind and sunlight into a form useable for modern applications requires massive capital investment in the form of both land and wind turbines and solar receiving equipment. This means that the energy that can be extracted from renewable sources, relative to that from conventional forms, by its very nature is limited and expensive.

Siting Limitations and Transmission Costs

Conventional power generation plants can be sited, in principle, almost anywhere, and such fuels as coal and natural gas can be transported to the generation facilities. This means that investment planning decisions can optimize transmission investment costs along with the other numerous factors that constrain and shape generation investment choices, among them land costs, environmental factors, reliability issues, transmission line losses, and the like. Wind and solar sites, on the other hand, must be placed where the wind blows and the sun shines with sufficient intensity and duration. (Photovoltaic installations, suitable for small applications, face the transmission problem either not at all or to a far smaller degree than solar thermal plants, but still are constrained by the intensity of sunlight.) Because appropriate sites are limited, with the most useful (i.e., lowest cost) ones exploited first, the successive (or marginal) cost of exploiting such sites must rise, so that even if wind and solar technologies exhibit important scale economies in terms of capacity and/or generation costs, scale economies may not characterize a broader cost calculation including the cost of finding and using particular sites. . . .

Because conventional generation investments can optimize transmission costs and other reliability factors more easily than is the case for wind and solar capacity, it would be surprising if such costs were not higher for the latter. This general condition is exacerbated by the physical realities that wind conditions are strongest in open plains regions, while solar generation in general requires regions with strong sunlight and, for thermal solar plants, sizeable open areas. For the U.S., the best wind capacity sites are in a region stretching from the northern plains down through Texas, and the best thermal solar sites are in the Southwest. The U.S. simply lacks significant east-west high-voltage interconnection transmission capacity to transport such power to the coast. . . .

Low Availability and Intermittency

Electric energy in large amounts cannot be stored at low cost in batteries due to technological limitations; only indirect storage in the form of water in dams is economical. This reality means that the production and consumption of electricity in a given power network must be balanced constantly in order to prevent blackouts, and more generally to preserve system reliability. Because unexpected surges in demand and/or outages of generating equipment can occur, backup generation capacity must be maintained; such backup capacity is termed the "operating reserve" for the given network. . . .

Electric supply systems respond to growing demands ("load") over the course of a day (or year) by increasing output from the lowest-cost generating units first, and then calling upon successively more expensive units as electric loads

US Electric Power Net Generation, Terawatt-Hours per Year

Source	2007	2012	2007–2012	2012 Mix
Coal	2,016	1,517	(499)	37.4%
Petroleum	79	34	(45)	0.8%
Natural Gas	897	1,231	334	30.3%
Nuclear	806	769	(37)	19.0%
Hydroelectric	261	286	25	7.0%
Biomass	56	58	2.0	1.4%
Geothermal	14.6	16.8	2.2	0.4%
Solar PV	0.6	4.3	3.7	0.1%
Wind	34	140	106	3.5%
Total	4,165	4,056	(109)	100%

TAKEN FROM: John Miller, "Which Government Policies and Other Factors Have Reduced US Carbon Emissions?," The Energy Collective, April 17, 2013.

grow toward the daily (or seasonal) peak. Because of the uncertainties caused by the unreliability of wind and sunlight, most electric generation capacity fueled by renewable energy sources cannot be assumed to be available upon demand; system planning and optimization cannot assume that such power will be available when it is expected to be most economical. Accordingly, it cannot be scheduled (or "dispatched"). Instead, it requires backup generation capacity to preserve system reliability.

And so the cost of that needed backup capacity becomes a crucial parameter usually not mentioned in public discussions of wind and solar power. One study, using figures from the California Independent System Operator, projects that an increase in California renewable generation capacity between 2009 and 2020 would be about 17.7 gigawatts (GW) for a 20 percent renewable requirement, and about 22.4 GW for the 33 percent requirement. The projected needs for backup capacity (of varying types) are, respectively, 0.8 GW (or 4.5 percent) and 4.8 GW (or 21 percent).

What would that backup power cost? U.S. wind and solar generation capacity in 2009 was about 34,000 MW. If we assume, conservatively, that this renewable capacity has required investment in backup capacity of about 3 percent (rather than 4.5 percent), that requirement would be about 1000 MW. Cost estimates published by the EIA suggest that this backup capacity has imposed fixed capital and operations and maintenance costs of about $1.7 billion, variable operating costs of approximately $2.00–$4.50 per megawatt-hour, and total costs per megawatt-hour of about $368.

That rough estimate is likely to be biased downward. Because state renewables requirements require system operators to take renewable power when it is available, conventional backup generation must be cycled—that is, in effect turned on and off—in coordination with the availability of the renewable generation. In particular for coal-fired generation, but also for gas combined-cycle backup generation, this means that the conventional assets cannot be operated as efficiently as would be the case were they not cycled up and down in response to wind or solar generation conditions. A recent study of the attendant emissions effects for Colorado and Texas found that requirements for the use of wind power impose significant operating and capital costs because of cycling needs for backup generation—particularly coal plants—and actually exacerbate air pollution problems.

The projected cost of renewable power in 2016 including the cost of backup capacity is at least five times higher than that for conventional electricity.

At the same time, outages of wind capacity due to weak wind conditions are much more likely to be correlated geographically than outages of conventional plants, for the obvious reason that weak winds in part of a given region are likely to be observed in tandem with weak winds in other parts of that region. Because appropriate regions for thermal solar sites and photovoltaic systems are concentrated geographically, the same correlation problem is likely to affect solar electric generation as well.

The higher cost of electricity generated with renewable energy sources is only one side of the competitiveness question; the other is the value of that generation, as not all electricity is created equal. In particular, power produced at periods of peak demand is more valuable than off-peak generation, whether during a given daily cycle or across annual seasons. In this context, wind generation in particular is problematic because in general there is an inverse relationship between the daily hours of peak demand and wind velocities, and between peak summertime demands and peak wintertime wind velocities: Winds tend to blow at night and in the winter. . . .

These realities suggest that the purported social benefits of policy support for renewables are illusory. Moreover, ongoing supply and price developments in the market for natural gas are likely to weaken further the competitive position of renewable power generation. At the same time, the subsidies and mandates that have been implemented in support of renewable electricity impose nontrivial costs upon the taxpayers and upon consumers in electricity markets. The upshot is the imposition of substantial net costs upon the U.S. economy as a whole even as the policies bestow important benefits upon particular groups and industries, thus yielding enhanced incentives for innumerable interests to seek favors from government. As has proven to be the case in most contexts, the outcomes of market competition, even as constrained and distorted by tax and regulatory policies, are the best guides for the achievement of resource allocation that is most productive.

"Even if conditions are poor for wind or
solar energy generation in one area on
a given day, a few hundred miles away
the winds could be blowing steadily and
the sun shining."

Alternative Energy Sources
Can Power the World by 2050

Louis Bergeron

*In the following viewpoint, Louis Bergeron cites a report pub-
lished by Stanford University researcher Mark Z. Jacobson and
University of California researcher Mark Delucchi, in which they
conclude that it would be possible to convert the entire world to
power from renewable sources by 2050. According to the report,
wind and water energy would meet 90 percent of the demand
for power, and other renewable sources such as hydroelectric
power would provide the rest. One of the benefits of the plan, the
report states, is that it will result in a 30 percent reduction in
world energy demand by converting combustion processes into
electrical or hydrogen fuel cell processes, which are more efficient.
Bergeron is a science writer at Stanford University's news service.*

Louis Bergeron, "The World Can Be Powered by Alternative Energy, Using Today's
Technology, in 20–40 Years, Says Stanford Researcher Mark Z. Jacobson," *Stanford
Report*, January 26, 2011. http://news.stanford.edu/news/2011/january/jacobson-world
-energy-012611.html. Copyright © 2011 by Stanford University News Service. All rights
reserved. Reproduced by permission.

6823772

As you read, consider the following questions:

1. According to the report cited by Bergeron, why do its authors believe that their plan would result in a 30 percent reduction in world energy demand?

2. How do the researchers think the unreliability of wind and solar power could be overcome?

3. How much of the world's land would be required for wind and solar power production under the plan proposed by the report?

If someone told you there was a way you could save 2.5 million to 3 million lives a year and simultaneously halt global warming, reduce air and water pollution and develop secure, reliable energy sources—nearly all with existing technology and at costs comparable with what we spend on energy today—why wouldn't you do it?

According to a new study coauthored by Stanford researcher Mark Z. Jacobson, we could accomplish all that by converting the world to clean, renewable energy sources and forgoing fossil fuels.

"Based on our findings, there are no technological or economic barriers to converting the entire world to clean, renewable energy sources," said Jacobson, a professor of civil and environmental engineering. "It is a question of whether we have the societal and political will."

He and Mark Delucchi, of the University of California, Davis, have written a two-part paper in *Energy Policy* in which they assess the costs, technology and material requirements of converting the planet, using a plan they developed.

The world they envision would run largely on electricity. Their plan calls for using wind, water and solar energy to generate power, with wind and solar power contributing 90 percent of the needed energy.

51

ORLAND PARK PUBLIC LIBRARY

Geothermal and hydroelectric sources would each contribute about 4 percent in their plan (70 percent of the hydroelectric is already in place), with the remaining 2 percent from wave and tidal power.

Vehicles, ships and trains would be powered by electricity and hydrogen fuel cells. Aircraft would run on liquid hydrogen. Homes would be cooled and warmed with electric heaters—no more natural gas or coal—and water would be preheated by the sun.

Commercial processes would be powered by electricity and hydrogen. In all cases, the hydrogen would be produced from electricity. Thus, wind, water and sun would power the world.

Renewable Energy by 2050

The researchers approached the conversion with the goal that by 2030, all new energy generation would come from wind, water and solar, and by 2050, all preexisting energy production would be converted as well.

"We wanted to quantify what is necessary in order to replace all the current energy infrastructure—for all purposes—with a really clean and sustainable energy infrastructure within 20 to 40 years," said Jacobson.

One of the benefits of the plan is that it results in a 30 percent reduction in world energy demand since it involves converting combustion processes to electrical or hydrogen fuel cell processes. Electricity is much more efficient than combustion.

That reduction in the amount of power needed, along with the millions of lives saved by the reduction in air pollution from elimination of fossil fuels, would help keep the costs of the conversion down.

"When you actually account for all the costs to society—including medical costs—of the current fuel structure, the costs of our plan are relatively similar to what we have today," Jacobson said.

ORLAND PARK PUBLIC LIBRARY

One of the biggest hurdles with wind and solar energy is that both can be highly variable, which has raised doubts about whether either source is reliable enough to provide "base load" energy, the minimum amount of energy that must be available to customers at any given hour of the day.

Jacobson said that the variability can be overcome.

"The most important thing is to combine renewable energy sources into a bundle," he said. "If you combine them as one commodity and use hydroelectric to fill in gaps, it is a lot easier to match demand."

Wind and solar are complementary, Jacobson said, as wind often peaks at night and sunlight peaks during the day. Using hydroelectric power to fill in the gaps, as it does in our current infrastructure, allows demand to be precisely met by supply in most cases. Other renewable sources such as geothermal and tidal power can also be used to supplement the power from wind and solar sources.

"One of the most promising methods of insuring that supply matches demand is using long-distance transmission to connect widely dispersed sites," said Delucchi. Even if conditions are poor for wind or solar energy generation in one area on a given day, a few hundred miles away the winds could be blowing steadily and the sun shining.

"With a system that is 100 percent wind, water and solar, you can't use normal methods for matching supply and demand. You have to have what people call a supergrid, with long-distance transmission and really good management," he said.

Another method of meeting demand could entail building a bigger renewable-energy infrastructure to match peak hourly demand and use the off-hours excess electricity to produce hydrogen for the industrial and transportation sectors.

Using pricing to control peak demands, a tool that is used today, would also help.

Ample Material and Land

Jacobson and Delucchi assessed whether their plan might run into problems with the amounts of material needed to build all the turbines, solar collectors and other devices.

They found that even materials such as platinum and the rare earth metals, the most obvious potential supply bottlenecks, are available in sufficient amounts. And recycling could effectively extend the supply.

"For solar cells there are different materials, but there are so many choices that if one becomes short, you can switch," Jacobson said. "Major materials for wind energy are concrete and steel and there is no shortage of those."

Jacobson and Delucchi calculated the number of wind turbines needed to implement their plan, as well as the number of solar plants, rooftop photovoltaic cells, geothermal, hydroelectric, tidal and wave energy installations.

They found that to power 100 percent of the world for all purposes from wind, water and solar resources, the footprint needed is about 0.4 percent of the world's land (mostly solar footprint) and the spacing between installations is another 0.6 percent of the world's land (mostly wind turbine spacing), Jacobson said.

One of the criticisms of wind power is that wind farms require large amounts of land, due to the spacing required between the windmills to prevent interference of turbulence from one turbine on another.

"Most of the land between wind turbines is available for other uses, such as pasture or farming," Jacobson said. "The actual footprint required by wind turbines to power half the world's energy is less than the area of Manhattan." If half the wind farms were located offshore, a single Manhattan would suffice.

Jacobson said that about 1 percent of the wind turbines required are already in place, and a lesser percentage for solar power.

"This really involves a large-scale transformation," he said. "It would require an effort comparable to the Apollo moon project or constructing the interstate highway system."

"But it is possible, without even having to go to new technologies," Jacobson said. "We really need to just decide collectively that this is the direction we want to head as a society."

| "Here's the bottom line: Renewables will remain niche players in the global energy mix for decades to come."

Don't Count Oil Out

Robert Bryce

In the following viewpoint, Robert Bryce argues that world demand for energy will continue to rise, and for the foreseeable future the demand can be met only by oil and gas, since there is no other source that can yield nearly as much energy. Renewable sources are much more expensive, he says, and even if they were inexpensive, it would take a long time to make the transition to renewables. He argues that a huge amount of money has been invested in the power delivery systems that already exist, and there is an adequate supply of oil and gas for many decades; therefore, there is no urgent need to abandon them. Bryce is a senior fellow at the Manhattan Institute for Policy Research.

As you read, consider the following questions:

1. According to Bryce, why will global carbon dioxide emissions from use of fossil fuels continue to rise?

Robert Bryce, "Don't Count Oil Out." From Slate, October 14 © 2011 The Slate Group. All rights reserved. Used by permission and protected by the Copyright Laws of the United States. The printing, copying, redistribution, or retransmission of this Content without express written permission is prohibited.

2. For what three reasons will fossil fuels continue to be the main source of energy for many years to come?

3. According to Bryce, what is today's biggest competitor to renewable energy sources?

It's easy to pick the dominant environmental issue of the last decade. It has been the issue of climate change and what—if anything—the countries of the world can do to limit, or reduce, carbon dioxide emissions.

But during that same decade, global carbon dioxide emissions rose by 28.5 percent to some 33 billion tons. And by 2030, the International Energy Agency expects global carbon dioxide emissions to rise by another 21 percent to about 40 billion tons.

Carbon dioxide emissions will continue rising because hundreds of millions of people in places like Vietnam, Malaysia, and South Korea—and, of course, China and India—are transitioning to a modern lifestyle, complete with cars, TVs, and other manufactured goods. As they do so, they are using more energy. Specifically, they are using more hydrocarbons—coal, oil, and natural gas. And while lots of idealistic environmentalists and some policy makers argue that we should quit using carbon-based fuels and move to a global economy powered by nothing but renewables, the hard reality is that hydrocarbons are here to stay.

There are three reasons why hydrocarbons will continue to dominate the global energy mix for decades to come: cost, the slow pace of energy transitions, and scale.

Explaining the first issue is relatively easy. The global energy sector is by far the world's biggest industry, with more than $5 trillion per year spent finding, refining, and delivering energy of various forms to consumers. Renewable sources like wind and solar have their virtues, but they cannot compare with hydrocarbons when it comes to economics. A recent analysis by the Energy Information Administration [EIA] estimates that wind-generated electricity from onshore wind turbines costs $97 per megawatt-hour. That's about 50 percent more than the same amount of electricity generated by natural gas, which the EIA estimates costs $63. Offshore wind is even more expensive, coming in at $243 per megawatt-hour. The least expensive form of solar-generated electricity—the type generated by photovoltaic panels—costs $210, or more than three times as much as the juice produced by burning natural gas.

If renewable sources of energy were dramatically cheaper than hydrocarbons, then perhaps we could be more optimistic about their ability to capture a larger part of the global energy mix. But even if that were true, a wholesale change in our energy mix will take a long time. "There is one thing all energy transitions have in common: they are prolonged affairs that take decades to accomplish," wrote Vaclav Smil in 2008. Indeed, for 109 years after the signing of the Declaration of Independence, wood was the dominant source of energy in America. It wasn't until 1885—the year that Grover Cleveland was first sworn in as president—that coal finally surpassed wood as the largest source of energy in the United States. Coal remained king until 1950, when it was deposed by oil. "And the greater the scale of prevailing uses and conversions, the longer the substitutions will take." Smil, a polymath, prolific author on energy issues, and distinguished professor at the University of Manitoba, believes that while a "world without fossil fuel combustion is highly desirable . . . getting there will demand not only high cost but also considerable patience: coming energy transitions will unfold across decades, not years."

Advantages of Oil

Smil's point can be proven by looking at oil's share of U.S. primary energy consumption. According to the EIA, in 1949, oil provided 37 percent of America's total energy needs. In

2009, oil's share of U.S. primary energy stood at . . . 37 percent. Over the past six decades, uncounted billions of dollars have been spent on efforts to reduce our need for oil, yet petroleum has been remarkably persistent. Conspiracy theorists will, of course, blame Big Oil. But the conspiracy wasn't hatched in Houston or Detroit. It's a conspiracy of basic physics. Love it or hate it—and all of us love what oil provides even as we are continually taught to hate the oil companies— oil is a miraculous substance.

If petroleum didn't exist, we'd have to invent it. Nothing else comes close to oil when it comes to energy density, ease of handling, flexibility, convenience, cost, or scale. Electric vehicles may be the celebrity car *du jour*, but modern batteries are only slightly better than the ones that Thomas Edison developed. Gasoline has 80 times the energy density of the best lithium ion batteries.

A final point on energy transitions. Believe it or not, in 2009, renewable energy sources had a *smaller* share of U.S. primary energy than they did back in 1949. Sure, wind and solar have grown dramatically in recent years, but in 1949, renewables—almost all of it hydropower—provided 9.3 percent of the country's energy needs. In 2009, renewables—again, much of it supplied by hydropower—provided 8.2 percent of U.S. energy.

The third issue—scale—is seldom discussed. And for many people, it's likely the most difficult issue to comprehend. There's little mystery as to why that is so. We use a googol of units to measure energy: Oil is sold in barrels, tons, gallons, and liters. Natural gas is measured and sold in cubic meters, millions of BTUs [British thermal units], therms, dekatherms, and cubic feet. Coal comes in long tons and short tons, but its pricing depends on myriad other factors, including heat content, ash content, sulfur content, and most important: the distance between the coal mine and the power plant. Electricity is sold in kilowatt-hours but electricity terminology spans

Why We Use Fossil Fuels

We use hydrocarbons—coal, oil, and natural gas—not because we like them, but because they produce lots of heat energy, from small spaces, at prices we can afford, and in the quantities that we demand. And that's the absolutely critical point. The energy business is ruthlessly policed by the Four Imperatives: power density, energy density, cost, and scale. . . .

Over the past century or so, the United States has built a $14 trillion per year economy that's based almost entirely on cheap hydrocarbons. No matter how much the United States and the rest of the world may desire a move away from those fossil fuels, the transition to renewable sources of energy—and to no-carbon sources such as nuclear power—will take most of the twenty-first century and require trillions of dollars in new investment.

Robert Bryce, Power Hungry: The Myths of "Green" Energy and the Real Fuels of the Future. *New York: Public Affairs, 2010.*

other units like volts, amperes, and ohms. Add in joules, watts, ergs, calories, and BTUs, and things get even more complicated.

Global Energy Consumption

We need a simpler measure for global energy use, which now totals about 241 million barrels of oil equivalent per day. That sum is almost impossible to comprehend, but try thinking of it this way: It's approximately equal to the total daily oil output of 29 Saudi Arabias. (Since 1970, Saudi Arabia's oil production has averaged 8.2 million barrels per day.) And of those 29 Saudi Arabias, 25—about 210 million barrels of oil equivalent—come from hydrocarbons.

Furthermore, over the past decade alone, global energy consumption has increased by about 27 percent, or six Saudi Arabias. Nearly all of that new energy came from hydrocarbons.

Scientists and policy makers can claim that carbon dioxide is bad. We can talk about wind, solar, geothermal, hydrogen, and lots of other forms of energy production. But the question that too few people are willing to ask is this one: Where, how, will we find the energy equivalent of 25 Saudi Arabias and have it all be carbon free?

The hard reality is that we won't. The Saudis have invested hundreds of billions of dollars over the past few decades drilling wells and building their infrastructure so that they can remain the world's most important oil exporter. And remember that all of those billions invested have given them exactly one Saudi Arabia, or about 3.4 percent of total global energy demand.

Taken together, the countries of the world have invested trillions of dollars in the energy- and power-delivery systems now in place. Smil explains this succinctly in his 2008 book, *Global Catastrophes and Trends.* "There is no urgency for an accelerated shift to a non–fossil fuel world: the supply of fossil fuels is adequate for generations to come; new energies are not qualitatively superior; and their production will not be substantially cheaper."

Smil's point about "cheaper" also affects the other issues at hand: the pace of energy transitions and scale. The biggest challenge for renewable energy in the United States is not the bad press associated with Solyndra or a lack of federal funding. Instead, it's the continuing avalanche of cheap natural gas, the fuel that competes most directly with wind and solar energy. Thanks to the shale revolution, which has transformed the U.S. oil and gas sector over the past three years, natural gas is now selling on the spot market at Henry Hub for less than $3.50 per million BTU. In October 2005, that same quantity of natural gas on the spot market was selling for more than $13.

Indeed, the United States now sits atop galaxies of low-cost gas that can be recovered from shale. In April, the Potential Gas Committee, a nonprofit group consisting of academics as well as representatives from government and industry, estimated U.S. gas resources at about 2,170 trillion cubic feet. At current rates of consumption, the United States likely has enough natural gas to last 90 years or more.

Here's the bottom line: Renewables will remain niche players in the global energy mix for decades to come. The past—and the foreseeable future—still belong to hydrocarbons. And we can expect natural gas, the cleanest of the hydrocarbons, to garner a bigger share of the global energy pie in the near term and in the long term.

Periodical and Internet Sources Bibliography

The following articles have been selected to supplement the diverse views presented in this chapter.

Claire Allen	"Our Role in the Future of Energy," *Christian Science Monitor*, November 9, 2010.
Richard Blackwell	"Green Energy Costs 'Minimal' for Consumers, Study Shows," *Globe and Mail* (Toronto, Canada), March 13, 2014.
The Hill	"Poll: Voters Want to Focus on Alternative Energy Growth," February 25, 2013.
Travis Hoium	"Renewable Energy Gaining on Fossil Fuels," *USA Today*, January 31, 2014.
Lou Kilzer	"Scientist: Renewable Energy Sources Won't Supplant Fossil Fuels by 2035," *Pittsburgh Tribune-Review*, October 27, 2013.
Stanley Reed	"Cracking the Energy Puzzles of the 21st Century," *New York Times*, October 14, 2013.
Joe Romm	"Renewables Projected to Add Triple the Capacity of New Fossil Fuel Plants by 2030," *ThinkProgress*, July 1, 2014.
Richard Schiffman	"Why the Shift to Alternate Energies Continues, Despite Shale Boom," Reuters, June 26, 2014.
John Waggoner	"Investing: Is This Alt Energy's Time in the Sun?," *USA Today*, September 6, 2013.
Matthew L. Wald	"New Energy Struggles on Its Way to Markets," *New York Times*, December 27, 2013.
Kathleen Hartnett White	"Fossil Fuels Offer Human Benefits That Renewable Energy Sources Can't Match," *Houston Chronicle*, June 21, 2014.

CHAPTER *2*

Do the Benefits
of Wind Power Outweigh
Its Disadvantages?

Chapter Preface

In May 2014, a federal court dismissed the last of twenty-six lawsuits that had, over a period of eleven years, stymied the development of Cape Wind, the first offshore wind farm in the United States, which is to be constructed in Nantucket Sound off the coast of Massachusetts. "The Cape Wind project is probably one of the most litigated energy projects in the U.S.," wrote Lewis Milford in the *Huffington Post*. "In the end, none of the claimed environmental harms was significant. None of them caused a judge to halt the work."

Offshore wind farms are common in Europe. The first one was built in 1991; as of January 2014, there were sixty-nine of them, and more are under construction. The largest so far is the London Array, with 175 turbines, which began operations in 2013 and can produce enough electricity to power half a million homes in the United Kingdom.

Offshore wind farms are extremely expense to build. However, the wind is stronger and more reliable offshore, especially in the late afternoon when the demand for power is strongest. Another advantage is that offshore wind farms can be sited close to crowded areas where the most power is needed, and once construction is complete they do not spoil nearby views or produce noise that disturbs residents.

Nevertheless, there has been strong opposition to offshore wind farms. In the case of Cape Wind, commercial fishermen who derive much of their income from Nantucket Sound fear that it will destroy their means of making a living. It will also restrict recreational and commercial boating. Local Native American tribes maintain that it will interfere with their traditional religious and cultural practices, which depend on an unobstructed view of the sun rising over Nantucket Sound. However, the strongest objections have come from local residents who believe that it will lower the value of their property and will be detrimental to the lucrative tourism industry.

"At night the project would look like LaGuardia Airport, complete with flashing red and amber lights and marked with foghorns," declares the website of the Alliance to Protect Nantucket Sound, a nonprofit organization that opposes Cape Wind and has filed many lawsuits in an attempt to prevent the wind farm's construction. "Its size and location would make it a major threat to the safety of air and sea travel in and around Nantucket Sound. Further, it would devastate commercial fishing in the Sound, desecrate a national treasure and sacred Tribal lands, and threaten endangered birds and marine mammals."

The Cape Wind project, which has now secured all required state and federal permits, will provide much of the power for Cape Cod and the islands of Nantucket and Martha's Vineyard. It will impose a $4 billion electric rate hike on Massachusetts ratepayers, the alliance warns, and yet it will do little or nothing to reduce carbon emissions, since backup fossil fuel plants must be available for times when the wind is not blowing.

Despite all the criticism, however, polls have shown that a majority of Massachusetts residents favor the Cape Wind project. Many deplore the long drawn-out delays caused by the multiple lawsuits aimed at stopping the project that have added considerably to its cost. At a time when most citizens support development of clean, renewable energy sources, the NIMBY (not in my back yard) attitude of those most closely affected is not shared by the general public.

Wind power has both advantages and disadvantages, and it is too soon to know what share of the world's energy needs it will fulfill in the future. The authors of the viewpoints in this chapter debate whether the benefits of wind energy outweigh its disadvantages.

> *"Wind is a native fuel that does not need to be mined or transported, taking two expensive costs out of long-term energy expenses."*

Wind Power Is Affordable and Has Low Environmental Impact

Windustry

In the following viewpoint, the nonprofit organization Windustry explains the many advantages of wind power—economical, social, and environmental. It also lists the disadvantages and states how advocates believe they can be overcome. Windustry contends that wind energy should be a cornerstone of a sustainable energy policy for the nation and potentially can supply more than 20 percent of the world's electricity. Windustry is a Minneapolis-based nonprofit that works throughout the United States to promote community-owned renewable energy.

As you read, consider the following questions:

1. According to Windustry, how does wind power contribute to the economy of rural areas?

Windustry, "Why Wind Energy?," Windustry.org. Copyright © by Windustry. All rights reserved. Reproduced by permission.

2. What effect do wind turbines have on agriculture, according to the viewpoint?

3. What is meant by "shadow flicker," and how frequently is it estimated to affect people living near wind turbines, according to the viewpoint?

In the U.S., the greatest source of human-caused greenhouse gas emissions is the power sector, at about 38%. The largest source of power is coal, which, even though it produces less than 40% of the power, produces over 70% of the power sector's greenhouse gas emissions. (20% of the greenhouse gas emissions are from natural gas–fired power plants.) Although wind turbines have become familiar in much of the U.S., wind power still (2013) only accounts for about 4% of the power sector.

The potential for wind energy is immense, and experts suggest wind power can easily supply more than 20% of U.S. and world electricity. The advantages and disadvantages of wind energy are detailed here to help you decide what the future of wind should be in the United States.

Economic Advantages

• *Revitalizes Rural Economies*: Wind energy can diversify the economies of rural communities, adding to the tax base and providing new types of income. Wind turbines can add a new source of property taxes in rural areas that otherwise have a hard time attracting new industry. Each 100 MW [megawatt] of wind development in southwest Minnesota has generated about $1 million per year in property tax revenue and about $250,000 per year in direct lease payments to landowners.

• *Fewer Subsidies*: All energy systems are subsidized, and wind is no exception. However, wind receives considerably less than other forms of energy. According to *Renewable Energy World* magazine, conventional energy receives US$300 billion in subsidies per year, while renewable energy has received less than US$20 billion of taxpayers' money in the last 30 years. A study published by researchers at Harvard in 2011 found that the full life-cycle cost of coal power is between about 9.5 and 27 cents per kilowatt-hour [kWh], most of which is paid by taxpayers in the form of increased health-related costs. These "indirect" subsidies amount to between $175 billion and over $500 billion/year. . . .

• *Free Fuel*: Unlike other forms of electrical generation where fuel is shipped to a processing plant, wind energy generates electricity at the source of fuel, which is free. Wind is a native fuel that does not need to be mined or transported, taking two expensive costs out of long-term energy expenses.

• *Price Stability*: The price of electricity from fossil fuels and nuclear power can fluctuate greatly due to highly variable mining and transportation costs. Wind can help buffer these costs because the price of fuel is fixed and free.

• *Promotes Cost-Effective Energy Production*: The cost of wind-generated electricity has fallen from nearly 40 cents per kWh in the early 1980s to 2.5–5 cents per kWh today depending on wind speed and project size.

• *Creates Jobs*: Wind energy projects create new short- and long-term jobs. Related employment ranges from meteorologists and surveyors to structural engineers, assembly workers, lawyers, bankers, and technicians. Wind energy creates 30% more jobs than a coal plant and 66% more than a nuclear power plant per unit of energy generated.

Social Advantages

• *National Security/Energy Independence*: Wind turbines diversify our energy portfolio and reduce our dependence on foreign fossil fuel. Wind energy is homegrown electricity and can help control spikes in fossil fuel cost. Distributed generation facilities, like many community wind projects, provide a safeguard against potential terrorist threats to power plants.

The Source of Wind

Wind energy, like most other types of *renewable energy*, gets its power from the sun. Even our so-called *fossil fuels*—coal, oil, and natural gas—derive their energy from the sun indirectly, since they were formed from the remains of ancient plants that needed sunlight to grow.

Most of the sun's energy reaches us as heat or light, but about 1%–2% of it becomes wind energy. That's about 50–100 times more energy than all the plants in the world capture from the sun.

Wind is created when solar radiation heats up the earth's land and water at different rates and at different times. For example, the air above land gets hotter faster than the air above water. Warm air is lighter in weight compared to cold air, which is denser. So the warm air on land rises into the sky, as much as six miles up, then begins to spread toward the north and south. Cooler air over the water rushes in to take its place, and that's what we call wind.

Rebecca L. Busby, Wind Power:
The Industry Grows Up. *Tulsa, OK: Penn Well, 2012.*

• *Supports Agriculture*: It is not often a new crop emerges from thin air. Wind turbines can be installed amid cropland without interfering with people, livestock, or production.

• *Local Ownership*: A significant contribution to the worldwide energy mix can be made by small clusters of turbines or even single turbines, operated by local landowners and small businesses. Developing local sources of electricity means we import less fuel from other states, regions, and nations. It also means our energy dollars are plowed back into the local economy.

Environmental Advantages

• *Conserves and Keeps Water Clean*: Turbines produce no particulate emissions that contribute to mercury contamination in our lakes and streams. Wind energy also conserves water resources. For example, producing the same amount of electricity can take about 600 times more water with nuclear power than wind, and about 500 times more water with coal than wind.

• *Clean Air*: Other sources of electricity produce harmful particulate emissions, which contribute to global climate change and acid rain. Wind energy is pollution free.

• *Negligible Greenhouse Gases*: The sources of most of our power, coal and natural gas, produce large quantities of greenhouse gases. (Coal much more than natural gas.) Wind power produces none, other than in the manufacture, installation and maintenance of the turbines. On average, those greenhouse gases are offset by the clean power the turbines produce within 9 months of operation.

• *Mining & Transportation*: Harvesting the wind preserves our resources because there is no need for destructive resource mining or fuel transportation to a processing facility.

• *Land Preservation*: Wind farms are spaced over a large geographic area, but their actual "footprint" covers only a small portion of the land resulting in a minimum impact on crop production or livestock grazing.

Disadvantages

• *A Variable Resource*: Turbines produce electricity only when the wind blows. This variability is monitored and compensated in the same way utilities monitor demand changes each day, so there are not any actual changes in power supply for the end users.

• *Aesthetics*: People have widely varied reactions to seeing wind turbines on the landscape. Some people see graceful symbols of economic development and environmental progress or sleek icons of modern technology. Others might see industrial encroachment in natural and rural landscapes. There are many ways to minimize the visual impact of wind turbines, including painting them a neutral color, arraying them in a visually pleasing manner, and designing each turbine uniformly.

• *Shadow Flicker*: Shadow flicker occurs when the blades of the rotor cast a shadow as they turn. Research has shown the worst-case conditions would affect, by way of light alteration, neighboring residents a total of 100 minutes per year, and only 20 minutes per year under normal circumstances. Designers of wind farms avoid placing turbines in locations where shadow flicker would be a problem for any significant amount of time.

• *Sound*: Wind turbines are not silent. The sounds they produce are typically foreign to the rural settings where wind turbines are most often used, but as turbine technology has improved over the years, the amount of sound has fallen considerably. The sounds of wind turbines do not interfere with normal activities, such as quietly talking to one's neighbor.

• *Biological Resource Impacts*: As with any construction project or large structure, wind energy can impact plants and animals, depending on the sensitivity of the area. Loss of wildlife habitat and natural vegetation are the primary wildlife concerns associated with wind energy. With modern turbines, mounted on tubular towers and whose blades spin only about 15 times per minute, bird collisions are now rare. Extensive environmental impact analysis is an integral part of project development to mitigate impacts as much as possible. The [National] Audubon Society and Sierra Club both support wind energy development, because the environmental advantages far outweigh the disadvantages.

• *Construction*: Wind systems can involve the transportation of large and heavy equipment. This can cause a large temporarily disturbed area near the turbines. Erosion is another potential environmental problem that can stem from construction projects. The single most reliable technique for limiting erosion is to avoid grading roads and to perform site reclamation post construction.

• *Radar*: Radar interference by wind turbines is rare and easily avoided through technological improvements and proper siting of turbines that are close to sensitive areas. A number of U.S. government installations have both wind turbines and functional radar, and the British military has a track record of successfully addressing these challenges.

For the sake of the planet, national security, rural economic revitalization, and resource preservation, we must promote a renewable energy economy. Wind power can be a cornerstone of that sustainable energy future because it is affordable, provides jobs, substantial and distributed revenue, and treads lightly on our environment without causing pollution, generating hazardous wastes, or depleting natural resources. Embracing wind energy today will lay the foundation for a healthy tomorrow.

"Attacks on wind projects from within the environmental movement threaten efforts to slow climate change and achieve energy independence."

Wind Farms Creating an Environmental Divide

Erin Ailworth

In the following viewpoint, Erin Ailworth describes how some environmentalists have come to oppose wind power, even though it is clean and renewable. Ailworth explains that individuals who live in rural areas because they want to be close to nature have found that bulldozing for the construction of wind turbines destroys the beauty of the land and that noise from the turbines spoils the pleasure of their chosen lifestyle. She says that advocates who worry about greenhouse gas emissions from the use of fossil fuels are concerned that the split within the environmental movement may lead to a delay in the achievement of clean energy goals. Ailworth is a reporter for the Boston Globe.

Erin Ailworth, "Wind Farms Creating an Environmental Divide." From *The Boston Globe*, August 11 © 2013 Boston Globe. All rights reserved. Used by permission and protected by the Copyright Laws of the United States. The printing, copying, redistribution, or retransmission of this Content without express written permission is prohibited.

As you read, consider the following questions:

1. According to Ailworth, what similar arguments are used by both advocates of wind power and advocates of natural gas?

2. What health problems have residents of Massachusetts experienced from wind turbines near their homes, according to the viewpoint?

3. According to the viewpoint, how many homes will be provided power by the nineteen wind turbines at the Hoosac Wind project?

Timothy Danyliw is the type of guy whose truck has a "No farms, no food" bumper sticker, who owns a T-shirt proclaiming "Renewable energy is American security," and who moved into a weathered, wood-framed house in the Berkshires for a quiet life amid nature.

His friend Larry Lorusso, a river guide and photographer, is much the same. His car runs on biodiesel, he's a fan of solar panels, and he heats his home with wood gathered from the forest around his house.

Yet these men, whose lifestyles embrace the environmental ethic, have found themselves at odds with environmental leaders who say that wind power is good for them—clean, sustainable energy that reduces dependence on fossil fuels and lowers greenhouse gas emissions. After watching bulldozers create access roads and clearings into 75 acres of wilderness, and living with the low roar of the industrial-sized turbines erected on ridges above their homes, Danyliw, Lorusso, and some of their neighbors have other ways to describe wind energy.

"It's similar to smoking," Danyliw said. "Smoking used to be advertised as good for your health."

"Carbon footprint, big time," added Lorusso.

Such descriptions echo the rhetoric long used by the green establishment to fight power plants and other development, and it's causing consternation among environmental and political leaders who have embraced wind power as a key component of renewable energy agendas. In November, Vermont governor Peter Shumlin warned in a speech that attacks on wind projects from within the environmental movement threaten efforts to slow climate change and achieve energy independence.

"If we let those voices that are our own divide us, we will continue to be the [energy] laggards rather than the leaders," Shumlin said at an event hosted by the New England Clean Energy Council, a trade group. "The stakes have never been higher."

Conflict Among Environmentalists

Many environmental leaders say their support for renewable energy projects depends on proper planning and construction, but their arguments for industrial-scale wind power can sound similar to those used by companies drilling for natural gas: America needs the energy, it's domestically produced, and it's cleaner than many alternatives.

Sue Reid, Massachusetts director of the Conservation Law Foundation, a Boston-based environmental advocacy group, said wind projects need to be responsibly sited, but they are essential to cutting pollution that contributes to climate change.

"You need to get energy from somewhere, right? So, no energy source has zero impact, but comparatively speaking, wind has far fewer impacts than fossil fuel generation," Reid said.

"They're not even in the same ballpark, and you can't disregard that context when looking at any wind project."

Massachusetts, with ambitious goals to reduce greenhouse gases, has aggressively pursued wind energy and other renewable sources. Installed wind energy generation has more than doubled over the past two years, to 103 megawatts, and Governor Deval Patrick wants that to increase to 2,000 megawatts by the beginning of the next decade. State officials estimate that's enough to power about 800,000 homes.

But the projects have stirred opposition from western Massachusetts to the Boston suburbs to Cape Cod, where residents have long fought the offshore Cape Wind project, which they say will mar views of Nantucket Sound and damage marine habitats. In Scituate, Falmouth, and Kingston, residents have complained that noisy turbines close to their homes cause headaches and dizzy spells, and interrupt sleep.

Research is still ongoing into the health effects of living near wind turbines.

In response, the state has undertaken noise studies while developing regulations, including acoustic policies, siting guidelines, and monitoring practices, to help communities decide whether wind energy is right for them.

The Hoosac Wind Project

Along the road southeast from North Adams toward the town of Florida, the 334-foot-tall wind turbines of the state's biggest wind farm peek above tree tops lining Bakke Mountain and Crum Hill, overlooking Route 2. From the road, the blades can be seen spinning methodically, appearing silent and innocuous.

Atop the ridge, it's obvious why Oregon-based Iberdrola Renewables, the project's developer, chose this site. The wind tugs at clothes and tightly cinched hard hats, rushing through the swirling turbine blades with the sound of an airliner passing overhead at 30,000 feet.

"Good place for a wind farm," Iberdrola spokesman Paul Copleman said as he toured the project with visitors.

The 28.5 megawatt Hoosac Wind project broke ground in 2011, and began operations in December—roughly a decade

Wind Turbine Syndrome

The most distinctive feature of wind turbine syndrome is the group of symptoms I call *visceral vibratory vestibular disturbance* [VVVD]. The adults who experience this describe a feeling of internal pulsation, quivering, or jitteriness, accompanied by nervousness, anxiety, fear, a compulsion to flee or check the environment for safety, nausea, chest tightness, and tachycardia. The symptoms arise day or night, interrupting daytime activities and concentration and interrupting sleep. Wakefulness is prolonged after this type of awakening. Subjects observe that their symptoms occur in association with specific types of turbine function: the turbines turned directly towards or away from them, running particularly fast, or making certain types of noise. The symptoms create aversive reactions to bedroom and house. Subjects tend to be irritable and frustrated, especially over the loss of their ability to rest and be revitalized at home. Subjects with VVVD are also prone to queasiness and loss of appetite even when the full set of symptoms is not present.

Nina Pierpont, Wind Turbine Syndrome: A Report on a Natural Experiment. *Santa Fe, NM: K-Selected Books, 2009.*

after it was first proposed. The 19 turbines are capable of producing enough power for an estimated 6,000 homes.

Florida and neighboring Monroe own some of the land the turbines sit on, meaning the towns will collect millions in lease payments and other revenue over the next few decades. Some residents like the wind farm, seeing it as a step toward energy independence and a cleaner environment, not to mention a needed source of revenue for these small, rural communities.

But ask others living along the base of the ridges. They'll talk of how land was bulldozed and blasted. A shift in the wind, they say, will send the turbines' jet engine–like noise streaming down.

The closest house, on Bliss Road, sits 1,650 feet or 0.3 miles from a turbine.

Lorusso, who guides visitors on river rafting trips, said he recognizes that wind power proponents are puzzled by opposition to projects like Hoosac, which they view as a clean, renewable, and endless resource. But Lorusso sees the turbines as interlopers in a wilderness landscape where "the sounds of civilization are few and far between" and the moon lights up a "cosmic sky at night."

"It doesn't make sense to me to wreck nature in order to save nature," Lorusso added. "It was a natural place. It was beautiful, and it has been wrecked now."

Benefits vs. Risks

Environmental advocates say they remain frustrated by what they see as a "not in my backyard mentality," despite a widely recognized need to reduce the use of fossil fuels. But even the environmental establishment has struggled to balance benefits against risks, particularly when renewable technologies threaten other priorities, such as protecting birds or marine life, said Salo Zelermyer, an environmental attorney at the law firm Bracewell & Giuliani LLP and former senior counsel for the Department of Energy.

"What you've seen is that a lot of environmentalists, while talking a good game about wind and solar, have oftentimes opposed large-scale wind turbine development," Zelermyer said. "What you have left is actually a very small sliver of sources for energy to turn your lights on."

Lorusso's friend, Danyliw, a semiretired photographer, moved to the Berkshires five years ago, seeking a quieter life.

But soon after the wind turbines started operating, he said, he began experiencing headaches and ringing in his ears.

Danyliw, who originally favored the Hoosac project, said he was once a big supporter of wind power. He pointed to his T-shirt depicting men raising a wind turbine, à la Marines raising the American flag at Iwo Jima. Today, he says, he wears the shirt ironically.

"I still believe that renewables are a great idea, but you can't destroy people's lives," he said. "This is like a highway came down and my house is stuck in the median. I chose to live in a quiet place, a healthy place and [Hoosac wind farm] took that away from me."

> "Wind turbine–related noise is not an issue that can be swept under the carpet by wind farm developers: Objectively noise should not be an issue, but subjectively it is."

The Noise of Wind Turbines Does Not Damage Human Health

Zoë Casey

In the following viewpoint, Zoë Casey discusses the arguments that have been advanced against wind power on the grounds of noise made by the turbines. Current wind turbines are less noisy than older ones; however, she says, the noise is very difficult to measure because it is always mixed with other sounds. Even though studies have shown that wind turbine noise is not harmful, people are convinced that it is. Therefore, she says, it is important for developers to be involved with the community and its leaders during the planning and construction of a wind power project. Casey is a writer for Wind Directions, *the European wind industry magazine.*

Zoë Casey, "Wind Farms: A Noisy Neighbour?," *Wind Directions*, February 2013. Copyright © 2013 by Zoë Casey. All rights reserved. Reproduced by permission.

As you read, consider the following questions:

1. According to Casey, what two kinds of noise are produced by wind turbines?

2. Why are today's wind turbines less noisy than those built in the past, according to the viewpoint?

3. According to Casey, what evidence has shown that wind turbine noise does not damage hearing?

Wind turbine noise is an issue fraught with emotion. Noise often comes up as a complaint from local wind turbine opposition groups and it is clearly something that wind turbine manufacturers, designers and developers alike must face up to, even if a vast body of [evidence] exists to show that there are no effects on human health from wind turbine noise.

In amongst the complaints that noise might ruin a good night's sleep, what are the real issues, how big are they in reality, and what can be done about them?

Noise emanating from wind turbines comes from two principal sources, Stefan Oerlemans, an engineer at Siemens, speaking at an EWEA [European Wind Energy Association] technology workshop on noise held in Oxford in December [2012], said. "There is the mechanical noise from the turbine's nacelle caused by the gearbox and generator, and there is the aerodynamic noise from the wind turbine's blade," he explained. "The dominant of these two sources is the blade, mainly during the blade's downwards stroke during a rotation," he said.

As blade lengths have increased over the years—a wind turbine rotor is now bigger than the wingspan of a Boeing 747 and turbines have grown from 200 kw [kilowatt] power ratings up to 7.5 MW [megawatt]—then the potential for greater noise levels goes up too. However, since the earlier days of modern wind power, turbine blade designs have improved drastically.

Designs of earlier modern turbines were inspired by 1930s aircraft designs, Oerlemans said. But today blades are custom made with much thinner trailing edge designs and aerodynamic blade tip designs—both of which make the blade much more slender and less noisy as it cuts the air.

Some designers have also started to explore "add-on" concepts, such as attaching extra features to a blade to further streamline its movement, although this approach is very sensitive to local conditions and can be a success or failure, he said.

"Blades undergo acoustic wind tunnel testing to find the right designs: Many noise sources can be suppressed by good design," Oerlemans stated.

Noise from the nacelle is easier to reduce and can be achieved by adding greater nacelle insulation, he added.

Noise, What Noise?

While wind turbine noise from the outset might seem like something scientific that can be measured categorically, it is a highly complex process once 'in the field'. "Measuring noise is very frustrating, especially in residential areas where background noise is very similar," Andy McKenzie, from Hayes McKenzie Partnership, said.

Wind turbine noise can be intermingled with the noise of rainfall, geographical water features, the sound of gravel crunching under car tyres, the wind blowing through the trees, farm yard noises and—one of the biggest annoyances to measurement—the noise of passing traffic. "All these and other sources affect the results," McKenzie said.

What is more, it is impossible to measure everywhere. Places like people's back gardens—and if we're talking about noise affecting public opinion this is surely a key place to measure—are usually off-limits. And there is the effect of the wind direction over the noise survey period—are the measurement instruments downwind from the wind farm?—he added.

"Simply put, background noise is very similar to turbine noise," McKenzie stated.

So, if we know that turbines do produce some noise, particularly as the blades swoop down, but we don't really know accurately how much noise they create in a given setting, what is the argument against wind turbines when it comes to noise?

Do Wind Turbines Impact Human Health?

"Sound from wind turbines does not pose a risk of hearing loss or other direct adverse health impacts," Mark Bastasch, from the Canadian Wind Energy Association (CanWEA), told delegates at the December EWEA noise workshop.

He pointed to 17 different peer-reviewed studies which back up his statement, available on the CanWEA website. In addition to those studies, there are many more: In 2010 the Australian government National Health [and] Medical Research Council concluded that, "there are no direct pathological effects from wind farms and that any potential impact on humans can be minimised by following existing planning guidelines." In January 2012 a study for the Massachusetts Department of Public Health said: "there is insufficient evidence that noise from wind turbines is directly . . . causing health problems or disease.". . .

As Robert Hornung, president of CanWEA, put it: "Wind has been attacked by opponents on the grounds that it is harmful to human health. This is despite the fact that the balance of scientific evidence clearly shows that wind turbines do not adversely affect human health, and in fact, wind energy is broadly recognised to be one of the safest forms of electricity generation available today."

However, it goes without saying that wind turbine–related noise is not an issue that can be swept under the carpet by

Little Noise from Wind Turbines

Wind plants are always located where the wind speed is higher than average, and the "background" noise of the wind tends to "mask" any sounds that might be produced by operating wind turbines—especially because the turbines only run when the wind is blowing. The only occasional exception to this general rule occurs when a wind plant is sited in hilly terrain where nearby residences are in dips or hollows downwind that are sheltered from the wind—in such a case, turbine noise may carry further than on flat terrain.

"Facts About Wind Energy and Noise,"
American Wind Energy Association.

wind farm developers: Objectively noise should not be an issue, but subjectively it is—and it is often a cause of concern for communities surrounding a wind farm even before the farm is up and running.

Involving the Community

Numerous opinion polls show that the public in general is in favour of renewable energy technologies like wind, but at a local level that support can wane without community engagement.

"Communication with the community is key," Tom Levy, manager of technical and utility affairs at CanWEA, explained. "You can have the strictest regulation in the world but you won't prevent problems if you don't approach the community, engaging people before and after the project is built." CanWEA has developed a set of best practice guidelines aimed at helping wind farm developers involve the local community and listen to their health-related concerns, he added.

Levy's ideas include engaging local prominent people, such as a town mayor, to show them how wind turbine noise blends in with background noise. Local media are also "critical" Levy said, advising developers to go and meet editors of local papers, local radio show hosts and local TV presenters.

"Change is often controversial and wind farm projects will often meet with local opposition. Education is the most powerful tool, but developers must also show respect by answering questions and listening to fears," he said. "Wind farm developers want to be good neighbours," Jeremy Bass, senior technical manager at RES [Renewable Energy Systems], added.

And so, in short, it seems that yes, wind turbines make noise—some of which has been eliminated with modern turbine designs—and no, this noise does not impact human health. But that noise does exist, even if it is at a very similar level to general background noise even in rural areas, and therefore all those involved in a wind farm project cannot ignore it.

Respecting national regulations on distances from dwellings is one thing—noise regulation varies hugely from country to country the scope of which goes beyond this [viewpoint]—but the most effective solution—community engagement—is something that should be built into every wind farm project sited near a community from the planning and construction phases to the operational phase.

> *"There are very few places where the wind always blows, and, not surprisingly, hardly anybody lives near those mostly unpleasant places."*

Wind Power Is Unreliable, Expensive, and Disruptive

Norman Rogers

In the following viewpoint, Norman Rogers argues that the use of wind power does not make sense. In his opinion, it offers none of the benefits its advocates claim: It does not create many jobs; it does not work except when the wind is blowing; and the more it is used, the more expensive it becomes. Wind farms are being built only because of government subsidies, he says, and because special interest groups have promoted wind power through propaganda. Rogers is a senior policy advisor at the Heartland Institute, a Chicago-based think tank.

As you read, consider the following questions:

1. According to Rogers, why is it that the more common wind power is, the more expensive it becomes?

Norman Rogers, "Wind Power Fiasco: Call Your Congressman," *American Thinker*, November 23, 2012. Copyright © 2012 by American Thinker. All rights reserved. Reproduced by permission.

2. According to Rogers, why does putting turbines in a windy location not necessarily mean that they can supply wind power less expensively than if they were in a less windy area?

3. What is the only effective way to eliminate carbon dioxide emissions from generation of electricity, according to the viewpoint?

W ind power is a joke. It makes no sense—none, nada.

The wind power lobbyists say it creates jobs. Well I have a better way to make jobs based on the same principles: Let's train dogs to walk on treadmills to generate electricity. Think of all the jobs for dog trainers, dog food companies, and dog walkers. Think of all the jobs at dog retirement homes for dogs too old to work. Think about all the do-gooders collecting a salary for looking out for the welfare of the dogs. Think about the attorneys employed in filing class-action suits against dog exploiters. Think about the jobs in organizations opposing the use of genetically modified dogs. Dogs on treadmills are much better than windmills for creating jobs.

Okay, windmills are not absolutely useless. If you have no alternative because you live 20 miles from the nearest power line, then feel free to get a windmill. Don't forget the banks of storage batteries to keep your TV running when the wind isn't blowing.

Windmills don't work when the wind isn't blowing. The wind power lobbyists don't emphasize that point. There are very few places where the wind always blows, and, not surprisingly, hardly anybody lives near those mostly unpleasant places.

Somehow, the environmentalist love of windmills is seemingly without limit. If you bother an eagle—even pluck a feather from a dead eagle—you are looking at hard time in the federal pen. But if you operate wind turbines that kill eagles on an industrial scale, you don't have to worry. Eagle-killing windmills are specifically exempted from liability. Windmills trump our national symbol. Just don't pick up the eagle feathers under the windmills.

Government programs that subsidize well-connected industries at the expense of everyone else are not new. The Midwest is filled with ethanol manufacturing plants where a good part of the corn crop is turned into very expensive alcohol that is then burned up in cars, at the expense of those taxpayers who are not corn farmers or owners of ethanol factories. Like the wind power program, the ethanol program was originally justified on global warming grounds that later were shown to be phony.

That the original justification for a program turns out to be phony doesn't necessarily matter. If you have enough citizens sucking at the federal teat, you can keep any program going, no matter how silly and useless. Our federal government subsidizes rich people growing sugar beets and sugarcane even though sweet corn syrup can be produced at a cheap price that would be even cheaper if we weren't burning up a good portion of the corn crop. Our federal government even subsidizes environmental groups to sue the federal government—via the misnamed Equal Access to Justice Act.

The Expense of Wind Power

Wind power is expensive and disruptive. The expense is the capital cost of the windmills amortized over the electricity produced during the life of the windmill. The unpredictable nature of wind disrupts the electrical grid, increasing the need for backup plants that have to be ready at a moment's notice to take over for becalmed windmills. The more wind power you have, the more expensive and disruptive it becomes. If you have just a little bit of wind power, the current situation in most places, the backup plants, or spinning reserve, that is normally on the grid can handle the disruption. If you have a

A Wind Farm Developer's View of Wind Turbines

[The project is] huge, the size of two nuclear plants in output, enough to power a million homes. More than 2,000 turbines, each between 2 and 3 megawatts. The first 1,000 megawatts will be ready by 2011, and 1,000 each year or two after that.

And you'll do all this on your beautiful 68,000-acre ranch?

I'm not going to have the windmills on my ranch. They're ugly. The hub of each turbine is up 280 feet, and then you have a 120-foot radius on the blade. It's the size of a 40-story building.

T. *Boone Pickens as told to David Case, "Texas Oil Tycoon Tackles Renewable Energy," Fast Company, June 2008.*

lot of wind power, then you have to build special backup plants—some of which, at the margin, are almost always idle but still cost a lot of money. If you have a little bit of wind power, you can exploit the best places that have wind, near power lines and near markets for the electricity. If you want a lot of wind power, you have to start using locations far from power lines and far from markets, at much greater cost.

In short, wind power is not unlike a poison that makes you mildly ill in small doses but that will put you in the hospital in large doses.

Wind power gets really expensive when you add electricity storage. Fanatical greens demand 100% green. That means no backup plants burning fossil fuels. They want to store the electricity for use when the wind stops blowing. There is only one method of storing electricity that is affordable and efficient: pumped storage. Pumped storage requires two reservoirs at different altitudes and a reversible hydroelectric plant. Water is pumped up to store energy and is run down through the turbines to recover the stored energy. Less than 20% of the electricity is wasted in the round trip up and down the mountain. If your wind turbines are in Iowa, where there is a lot of wind but no mountains, you have to run power lines hundreds of miles to a location where you can build pumped storage plants. . . .

If it weren't for massive government subsidies and mandates, nobody would be building wind farms. The biggest subsidy in the subsidy tangle is the production tax credit. The government promises to pay, for the first 10 years of a windmill's life, 2.2 cents per kilowatt-hour, adjusted for inflation, for power generated by wind. This is scheduled to terminate at the end of 2012, and the wind energy lobby, opposed by underfinanced good government types, is lobbying to have it renewed.

Of course, the extremist environmental groups are in bed with the wind industry. Believers in global warming catastrophe should be aware that there is one really effective and proven way to get rid of CO_2 emissions from generating electricity: nuclear power. The environmental organizations killed nuclear power in the 1970s, though, so it is a bit difficult for them to now rediscover the virtues of nuclear power. Their alternative is wind power.

In the Pacific Northwest, at certain times, there is too much electricity between hydroelectric and wind. If the wind power companies can't sell their electricity, they can't get the 2.2-cent government subsidy. Their solution is a negative price for the electricity—they pay people to use their electricity. Of course, this then challenges the users of electricity to invent ways to waste electricity. Perhaps the government will outlaw paying people to waste electricity, in which case the payments will probably be disguised in some fashion.

So the next time someone mentions sustainable energy or green energy, be nice. Remember: They are probably just ill-informed due to the barrage of propaganda from special interests and ideological extremists pretending to be stewards of the earth.

| "*The pressure is now on for wind energy companies to reduce bird and bat mortality.*"

Wind Power Companies Are Making Extensive Efforts to Protect Birds

Roger Drouin

In the following viewpoint, Roger Drouin explains the various methods that are being made to prevent birds and bats from being killed by wind turbines. Many possible experimental schemes are being tried, from making the turbines less attractive to detecting the birds' approach and slowing or shutting down turbines when flocks are present. Drouin argues that the wind industry is committed to reducing dangers to wildlife, both to avoid trouble with the government and to appease people who work in that industry and care about the environment. Drouin is a journalist who covers environmental issues.

As you read, consider the following questions:

1. According to the viewpoint, what is the best way to prevent bird deaths from wind turbines?

Roger Drouin, "For the Birds (and the Bats): 8 Ways Wind Power Companies Are Trying to Prevent Deadly Collisions," *Grist*, January 3, 2014. Copyright © 2014 by Grist. All rights reserved. Reproduced by permission.

2. What usually kills the birds that die on wind farms, according to the viewpoint?

3. What experimental method cited by Drouin is being tried to prevent bat deaths from wind turbines?

Hundreds of thousands of birds and bats are killed by wind turbines in the U.S. each year, including some protected species such as the golden eagle and the Indiana bat. That's only a small fraction of the hundreds of millions killed by buildings, pesticides, fossil fuel power plants, and other human causes, but it's still worrying—especially as wind power is experiencing record growth.

Both the wind industry and the federal government have been under intense public scrutiny over the issue in recent weeks. In late November [2013], the [Barack] Obama administration fined Duke Energy Renewables $1 million for illegally killing birds, the first time a wind company has been prosecuted under the Migratory Bird Treaty Act.

Then, just two weeks later, the administration announced a controversial new rule that will allow energy companies to get 30-year permits for non-intentional eagle deaths at wind farms. The feds emphasize that the new rule requires additional conservation measures, but it still angered many conservationists.

The pressure is now on for wind energy companies to reduce bird and bat mortality. Lindsay North, outreach manager for the American Wind Energy Association, which lobbies for the industry, says wind developers are committed to "doing our best to try to have the lowest impact on birds."

The industry is collaborating with wildlife researchers on promising technologies and approaches that are already being field-tested, and on some experimental and even far-fetched ideas that could help reduce mortality in the long term.

"I am very optimistic we can make significant progress," said biologist Taber Allison, director of research at the American Wind Wildlife Institute, a nonprofit partnership of wind companies, scientists, and environmental organizations such as the National Audubon Society and the Sierra Club.

Here are eight things the industry is trying or considering in an effort to reduce bird and bat mortality.

Smarter Siting

It's all about location, location, location. The No. 1 way to prevent bird deaths is to do a better job choosing sites for wind energy development, said raptor researcher Richard Gerhardt: "It's an issue of where you put the turbines."

Federal wildlife officials, working with the industry, finalized more specific, stricter siting practices this year, as part of the same changes that allowed the 30-year permits for eagle deaths. In particular, federal officials are worried about the placement of wind farms in golden eagle habitats out West, and the new permitting process takes those concerns into account. When they are focused on their prey, golden eagles, which are protected under three federal laws, are especially vulnerable to turbines.

"Certainly as an industry we believe not every site is equal and not every site should be developed," said John Anderson, director of siting policy for AWEA [American Wind Energy Association]. "It starts with desktop analysis of where the risk lies," he said. "But you can't assess risks without on-the-ground boots analysis."

It would be difficult for wind developers to avoid eagle territory altogether. "The eagles love to fly where the wind is high and strong and they can soar over open country," said Frank B. Isaacs, golden eagle project manager for the Oregon Eagle Foundation. "And it is exactly the same places they want to put these wind farms."

But wind companies can at least avoid eagles' and hawks' migratory routes and known flight paths. For instance, wind farms could be set back from cliffs and sloping hills where eagles use an updraft to soar, Isaacs said.

Radar

The industry is also turning to radar technology that could detect when eagles and other birds are approaching. Turbines could be slowed or shut down when the radar, along with employees monitoring the horizon, determine birds are within a certain zone.

Some radar systems are proving to be better than others at telling an eagle from a crow (or a swarm of insects), said Anderson. But live testing has shown that the more refined radar technology can reduce the risk to large species, according to Allison, including protected birds such as whooping cranes, condors, and eagles.

This kind of early-warning radar technology has been deployed at wind farms along the Texas Gulf coast during the spring migration of songbirds. Some wind companies in the area are also watching for meteorological conditions that might suggest when songbirds are in migration, and conditions such as low visibility, when the songbirds might fly lower and thus closer to the turbines.

GPS Tracking

Thus far there have been no reported California condor deaths caused by wind turbines. And at least one company is trying to ensure the endangered birds can coexist with the growing wind energy presence in the state.

Many of the 230 California condors flying in the wild are fitted with GPS [global positioning system] transmitters, so Terra-Gen, one of the top wind developers in the country, uses a high-frequency receiver to track the condors near its California facilities.

"They are listening, if you will, for condors," Allison said. "If they pick up a signal and it gets within this space, the company can say, 'We'll shut down this string of turbines.'"

Ultrasonic Acoustics

Most birds killed by wind turbines die because they get hit by spinning blades. Many bats seem to die for a different, even gorier reason: the lower wind pressure near the blades causes their lungs to explode. Because birds and bats react differently to turbines, scientists are pursuing different methods to protect them.

"There are two things that appear to be the most promising" when it comes to reducing bat deaths, said Chris Hein, wind energy program coordinator with Bat Conservation International.

The first of those is ultrasonic acoustic determent. Bat Conservation International has been collaborating with Deaton Engineering to design ultrasonic "boom boxes" that emit continuous high-frequency sounds, from 10 kHz [kilohertz] to 100 kHz, intended to confuse bats' echolocation to the point that they avoid the area.

"It essentially jams their radar, making it difficult to perceive sonar," Hein said. "That creates a disorientating atmosphere, and they don't want to be associated with that airspace. It doesn't harm the bat in any way. It would be like going into an extremely bright room that is so bright we wouldn't be able to navigate or see well."

Study results on this kind of technology have been largely inconclusive so far, but Hein believes that's because of the inconsistency of the devices that have been used to date. There are encouraging signs, he said. Tests of some ultrasonic acoustic equipment have found that it can halve the number of fatalities for certain species of bats.

"We still have a long way to go with that technology," Hein said. For one thing, it needs to be refined to work better in rain and high wind.

But he's hopeful that recent advances could lead to commercially deployable devices.

Leaving Turbines Off When Wind Speeds Are Low

The second strategy that has been shown to help reduce bat deaths is waiting longer to turn on the turbines, until wind speeds are higher. "Bats like to travel in very low-wind conditions," Hein said.

According to the only published study on the subject, leaving the turbines dormant until wind speed reaches 5.5 meters per second reduced bat mortality by nearly 60 percent compared with normally operating turbines. The industry standard is to have blades start spinning when wind hits 3.5 to 4 meters per second.

The question is whether this method is economically feasible. Anderson said the industry is "in the process" of evaluating this strategy.

"It does come at a cost to the electric company," Hein said. "But some of the early research shows the loss of revenue is not that much."

This strategy is currently being employed at wind farms in the Midwest and on the East Coast within the habitat range of the Indiana bat, a medium-sized, mouse-eared bat listed as endangered since 1967.

Painting Turbines Different Colors

Some research has shown that migratory tree bats are attracted to turbines, but the reason isn't known, Allison said. One study found that they may associate the turbines with a body of water.

Another theory is that bats approach the turbines in pursuit of prey. A study conducted in England suggested that simply changing the color of wind turbines to hues less attractive to insects could reduce the number of bugs that congregate around the turbines, which could in turn reduce bat deaths.

Ultimately, understanding why bats keep coming to turbines will be key in finding ways to keep them safe.

Designing New Turbine Shapes

Earlier designs were found to attract roosting birds, which would perch and nest inside the turbines' lattice-style structures, but newer designs discourage roosting.

In addition, engineers are exploring completely new kinds of wind equipment that could potentially be less harmful to birds and bats than traditional turbines. They range from large kites that harness the wind to vertical axis turbines.

A jet engine–inspired design, called the FloDesign turbine, marks a distinct departure from traditional turbine design, with blades encased in a larger structure. Because it would be more visible, Allison believes it could pose less of a threat to birds.

Strike Detection

If a turbine could recognize when it has been hit by a bird, it could potentially slow itself down or shut off to minimize the risk to other birds in the area.

A collaborative research effort between Oregon State University and Mesalands Community College in New Mexico is looking into this idea. Researchers are currently using tennis balls to mimic bird strikes.

The research could lead to commercial strike-detection equipment, said Jim Morgan, director of the North American Wind Research and Training Center at Mesalands. "If it works, it could be helpful for offshore wind," said Allison.

Morgan is hopeful that the research at Mesalands and elsewhere will eventually lead to a notable reduction in bird and bat mortality. "Man is good at solving problems when someone is willing to invest in the science," he said.

Reducing wind development's impact on endangered species and other wildlife would help the industry avoid problems with the federal government and boost wind power's public image.

Allison believes there is also another motive: "They want to do it because they are conservation-minded, too. Many people in the wind industry work in the industry because they believe they're doing something to reduce the impacts of climate change, which many believe is the single biggest threat."

| "More than 573,000 birds are killed by the country's wind farms each year, including 83,000 hunting birds such as hawks, falcons and eagles."

The Government Is Allowing Wind Power Companies to Kill Too Many Eagles

Dina Cappiello

In the following viewpoint, Dina Cappiello reveals that although killing eagles is against the law, the government allows the wind energy industry to do it without penalty. A great many eagles have been killed or injured by wind turbines, but because wind power is a renewable source of energy that the government encourages, the companies that produce it receive favorable treatment compared to other industries. Furthermore, Cappiello explains that under a new rule, the industry will be given thirty-year permits to go on killing a limited number of eagles. She explains that this has created a division among environmentalists, many of whom formerly favored the wind energy industry. Cappiello is the national environmental reporter for the Associated Press in Washington, DC.

Dina Cappiello, "Wind Farms Get Pass on Eagle Deaths," Friends of Pocosin Lakes NWR (AP), May 14, 2013. Copyright © 2013 by Associated Press. All rights reserved. Reproduced by permission.

As you read, consider the following questions:

1. According to the viewpoint, why are members of Congress investigating the Obama administration's failure to prosecute wind energy companies for killing eagles?

2. According to Cappiello, how does the government justify allowing wind energy companies to kill eagles?

3. Why is it that flying eagles do not avoid wind turbines, according to the viewpoint?

Wind farms in this corner of Wyoming have killed more than four dozen golden eagles since 2009, one of the deadliest places in the country of its kind.

But so far, the companies operating industrial-sized turbines here and elsewhere that are killing eagles and other protected birds have yet to be fined or prosecuted—even though every death is a criminal violation.

The [Barack] Obama administration has charged oil companies for drowning birds in their waste pits, and power companies for electrocuting birds on power lines.

But the administration has never fined or prosecuted a wind energy company, even those that flout the law repeatedly.

"What it boils down to is this: If you electrocute an eagle, that is bad, but if you chop it to pieces, that is OK," said Tim Eicher, a former U.S. Fish and Wildlife Service enforcement agent based in Cody.

It's a double standard that some Republicans in Congress said Tuesday [in May 2013] they would examine after an Associated Press [AP] investigation revealed that the Obama administration has shielded the wind power industry from liability and helped keep the scope of the deaths secret.

"We obviously don't want to see indiscriminate killing of birds from any sort of energy production, yet the administration's ridiculous inconsistencies begs questioning and clarity—clarity on why wind energy producers are let off the hook," said Sen. David Vitter, R-La.

The House Natural Resources Committee, which was at the beginning stages of an investigation, vowed to dig deeper Tuesday.

"There are serious concerns that the Obama administration is not implementing this law fairly and equally," said Jill Strait, a spokeswoman for the committee's chairman, Rep. Doc Hastings, R-Wash.

Support for Wind Power

Wind power, a pollution-free energy intended to ease global warming, is a cornerstone of President Barack Obama's energy plan. His administration has championed a $1 billion-a-year tax break to the industry that has nearly doubled the amount of wind power in his first term.

"Climate change is really the greatest threat that we see to species conservation in the long run," said Fish and Wildlife Service director Dan Ashe in an interview with the AP on Monday. "We have an obligation to support well-designed renewable energy.". . .

The result is a green industry that's allowed to do not-so-green things.

More than 573,000 birds are killed by the country's wind farms each year, including 83,000 hunting birds such as hawks, falcons and eagles, according to an estimate published in March in the peer-reviewed *Wildlife Society Bulletin*.

Getting precise figures is impossible because many companies aren't required to disclose how many birds they kill. And when they do, experts say, the data can be unreliable.

When companies voluntarily report deaths, the Obama administration in many cases refuses to make the information public, saying it belongs to the energy companies or that revealing it would expose trade secrets or implicate ongoing enforcement investigations.

You know, I think I felt safer back when we were an Endangered Species.

© Lynda Barry/windtoons.com.

Nearly all the birds being killed are protected under federal environmental laws, which prosecutors have used to generate tens of millions of dollars in fines and settlements from businesses, including oil and gas companies, over the past five years. . . .

The large death toll at wind farms shows how the renewable energy rush comes with its own environmental consequences, trade-offs the Obama administration is willing to make in the name of cleaner energy.

"It is the rationale that we have to get off of carbon, we have to get off of fossil fuels, that allows them to justify this," said Tom Dougherty, a longtime environmentalist who worked for nearly 20 years for the National Wildlife Federation in the West, until his retirement in 2008. "But at what cost? In this case, the cost is too high." . . .

By not enforcing the law, the administration provides little incentive for companies to build wind farms where there are fewer birds. And while companies already operating turbines are supposed to avoid killing birds, in reality there's little they can do once the windmills are spinning.

Wind farms are clusters of turbines as tall as 30-story buildings, with spinning rotors as wide as a passenger jet's wingspan. Though the blades appear to move slowly, they can reach speeds up to 170 mph at the tips, creating tornado-like vortexes.

Flying eagles behave like drivers texting on their cell phones; they don't look up. As they scan for food, they don't notice the industrial turbine blades until it's too late.

The rehabilitation coordinator for the Rocky Mountain Raptor Program, Michael Tincher, said he euthanized two golden eagles found starving and near death near wind farms. Both had injuries he'd never seen before: One of their wings appeared to be twisted off.

"There is nothing in the evolution of eagles that would come near to describing a wind turbine. There has never been an opportunity to adapt to that sort of threat," said Grainger Hunt, an eagle expert who researches the U.S. wind power industry's deadliest location, a northern California area known as Altamont Pass. Wind farms built there decades ago kill more than 60 per year.

A Difficult Choice

Eagle deaths nave forced the Obama administration into a difficult choice between its unbridled support for wind energy and enforcing environmental laws that could slow the industry's growth. . . .

The Obama administration has proposed a rule that would give wind energy companies potentially decades of shelter from prosecution for killing eagles. The regulation is currently under review at the White House.

The proposal, made at the urging of the wind energy industry, would allow companies to apply for 30-year permits to kill a set number of bald or golden eagles. Previously, companies were only eligible for five-year permits.

In exchange for the longer timetable, companies agree that if they kill more eagles than allowed, the government could require them to make changes. But the administration recently said it would cap how much a company could be forced to spend on finding ways to reduce the number of eagles its facility is killing. . . .

That's because without a long-term authorization to kill eagles, investors are less likely to finance an industry that's violating the law.

Typically, the government would be forced to study the environmental effects of such a regulation before implementing it. In this case, though, the Obama administration avoided a full review, saying the policy was nothing more than an "administrative change."

"It's basically guaranteeing a black box for 30 years, and they're saying 'trust us for oversight.' This is not the path forward," said Katie Umekubo, a renewable energy attorney with the Natural Resources Defense Council and a former lawyer for the Fish and Wildlife Service. In private meetings with industry and government leaders in recent months, environmental groups have argued that the 30-year permit needed an in-depth environmental review.

The tactics have created an unexpected rift between the administration and major environmental groups favoring green energy that, until the eagle rule, had often been on the same side as the wind industry.

Those conservation groups that have been critical of the administration's stance from the start, such as the American Bird Conservancy, have often been cut out of the behind-the-scenes discussions and struggled to obtain information on bird deaths at wind farms. . . .

Last year, over objections from some of its own wildlife investigators and biologists, the Interior Department updated its guidelines and provided more cover for wind companies that violate the law.

The administration and some environmentalists say that was the only way to exact some oversight over an industry that operates almost exclusively on private land and generates no pollution, and therefore is exposed to little environmental regulation.

Under both the Migratory Bird Treaty Act and the Bald and Golden Eagle Protection Act, the death of a single bird without a permit is illegal.

But under the Obama administration's new guidelines, wind energy companies—and only wind energy companies—are held to a different standard. Their facilities don't face additional scrutiny until they have a "significant adverse impact" on wildlife or habitat. But under both bird protection laws, any impact has to be addressed. . . .

Experts working for the agency in California and Nevada wrote in government records in June 2011 that the new federal guidelines should be considered as though they were put together by corporations, since they "accommodate the renewable energy industry's proposals, without due accountability."

The Obama administration, however, repeatedly overruled its experts at the Fish and Wildlife Service. In the end, the wind energy industry, which was part of the committee that drafted and edited the guidelines, got almost everything it wanted.

"Clearly, there was a bias to wind energy in their favor because they are a renewable source of energy, and justifiably so," said Rob Manes, who runs the Kansas office for the Nature Conservancy and who served on the committee. "We need renewable energy in this country." . . .

No Simple Solution

At . . . Duke Energy's Top of the World wind farm, a 17,000-acre site with 110 turbines located about 35 miles east of Casper, 10 eagles have been killed in the first two years of operation. It is the deadliest of Duke's 15 wind power plants for eagles.

The company's environmental director for renewable energy, Tim Hayes, said Duke is doing all it can, not only because it wants to fix the problem but because it could reduce the company's liability. Two of the company's wind farms in Wyoming—Top of the World and Campbell Hill—are under investigation by the federal government for the deaths of golden eagles and other birds, according to a report the company filed with the Securities and Exchange Commission last week. The report was filed after the AP visited a Duke facility in Wyoming and asked senior executives about the deaths.

Duke encourages workers to drive slower so as not to scare eagles from their roosts. They remove dead animals that eagles eat. And they've removed rock piles where the birds' prey lives. They also keep internal data on every dead bird in order to determine whether these efforts are working. The company is also testing radar technology to detect eagles and is considering blaring loud noises to prevent the birds from flying into danger.

The only other option is shutting off the turbines when eagles approach. And even that method hasn't been scientifically proven to work.

At Top of the World, Duke shut down 13 turbines for a week in March, often the deadliest time for eagles. The experiment, the company says, paid off. Not a single eagle was killed that month.

Hayes says the company has repeatedly sought a permit from the federal government to kill eagles legally, but was told it was killing too many to qualify.

When an eagle is killed, Duke employees are also prohibited by law from removing the carcass.

Each death is a tiny crime scene. So workers walk out underneath the spinning rotors and cover the dead bird with a tarp. It lies there, protected from scavengers but decaying underneath its shroud, until someone from the government comes to get it.

> "The fear of property value loss persists and is exploited by anti-wind campaigning groups in their attempts to turn local populaces against wind developments."

Industrial Wind Turbines Do Not Hurt Property Values

Mike Barnard

In the following viewpoint, Mike Barnard states that many statistical studies, some of which he describes in detail, have shown that property values of homes are not reduced by nearby wind farms. In his opinion, the reliability of the few studies showing a reduction is open to question. Advocates of wind power need to respect people's emotional reactions, he says, because opponents use emotional appeals to motivate homeowners and organizations to fight against wind turbines. Barnard is a senior fellow at the Energy and Policy Institute.

As you read, consider the following questions:

1. According to Barnard, what is the most substantive study of the impact of wind turbines on home values?

Mike Barnard, "Property Values Not Hurt by Wind Energy," Energy and Policy Institute, March 26, 2014. Copyright © 2014 by Mike Barnard. All rights reserved. Reproduced by permission.

2. Why does Barnard feel that to say results of a home value study do not match observation of what is happening is not a valid objection to such studies?

3. According to the viewpoint, what is the main problem with the New York study that showed a decrease in value of property near wind turbines?

Ten major studies in three countries of 1.3 million property transactions over 18 years of data have found no connection between wind farms and property values. Yet the fear of property value loss persists and is exploited by anti-wind campaigning groups in their attempts to turn local populaces against wind developments.

By comparison, only two moderately reliable studies with some statistical significance found property value impacts, and they are both challenged in different ways. Five other often referenced studies are merely case studies with no statistical significance, done by appraisers who show strong evidence of bias, and in one case there is clear evidence that they ignored the reality of the property they appraised.

The evidence that wind farms don't harm property values is robust, methodologically sound and from reliable organizations. The evidence that wind farms harm property values is much weaker, methodologically challenged at best and usually from much less reliable organizations.

Whether it is a home or a vacation property, people who buy or own rural property have deep emotional drivers attached to it. For some older people, it is the home they have been in for decades. For others, it is a rural idyll, the fantasy of a hobby farm or country estate. For others, it is an escape from the vertical canyons, concrete, steel and noise of the city. For most of them, it represents a very large percentage of their finances, with all of the attendant concerns that it might turn to dust as happened in the US with the subprime mortgage collapse in 2008. It is worthwhile to respect the deep emotions involved in this subject. Anti-wind advocacy groups certainly do, and while some are directly motivated by fears of falling properties, many broader groups are using those fears to directly motivate grassroots organizations to form to fight wind turbines.

Property Values Show No Long-Term Correlation to Wind Turbine Presence

There have been several major reports released in 2013 and 2014 that substantially add to the evidence base for wind farms and property values. . . .

The most substantive is the 2013 update of the 2009 Lawrence Berkeley National Laboratory (LBNL) study, described below in detail.

To ensure that the seriousness of this organization and its devotion to academic excellence and scientific truth is understood, thirteen Nobel Prize winners have been associated with the lab and thirteen have been awarded the US National Medal of Science, the top US honor for lifetime achievements in science. Dozens more have received other extraordinary levels of recognition. This is an organization that is not for sale. This is an organization that takes its independence and excellence seriously, and accusations leveled at the studies it performs related to being bought and paid for by the wind industry are specious and without basis.

Pertinent points are extracted here:

We collected data from more than 50,000 home sales among 27 counties in nine states. These homes were within 10 miles of 67 different wind facilities, and 1,198 sales were within 1 mile of a turbine—many more than previous studies have collected. The data span the periods well before announcement of the wind facilities to well after their construction. We find no statistical evidence that home values near turbines were affected in the post-construction or post-announcement/pre-construction periods.

Transactions assessed covered geographically varied sites across the USA.

This major study controlled for significantly more variables and concerns than previous studies and found no impact on property values from wind farms.

The LBNL also collaborated with the University of Connecticut on an assessment of property value impacts near wind farms in the US state of Massachusetts in 2013, publishing their results in January 2014. They spread the net even wider:

> To determine if wind turbines have a negative impact on property values in urban settings, this report analyzed more than 122,000 home sales, between 1998 and 2012, that occurred near the current or future location of 41 turbines in densely populated Massachusetts communities.

> The results of this study do not support the claim that wind turbines affect nearby home prices. Although the study found the effects from a variety of negative features (such as electricity transmission lines and major roads) and positive features (such as open space and beaches) generally accorded with previous studies, the study found no net effects due to the arrival of turbines in the sample's communities. Weak evidence suggests that the announcement of the wind facilities had a modest adverse impact on home prices, but those effects were no longer apparent after turbine construction and eventual operation commenced. The analysis also showed no unique impact on the rate of home sales near wind turbines. . . .

Earlier Studies Showed Similar Results

The best study in this field prior to 2013 was funded by the US Office of Energy Efficiency and Renewable Energy. They mandated the Lawrence Berkeley National Laboratory to study the concern and the report was delivered in 2009. Here's what they found:

The present research collected data on almost 7,500 sales of single-family homes situated within 10 miles of 24 existing wind facilities in nine different U.S. states. The conclusions of the study are drawn from eight different hedonic pricing models, as well as both repeat sales and sales volume models. The various analyses are strongly consistent in that none of the models uncovers conclusive evidence of the existence of any widespread property value impacts that might be present in communities surrounding wind energy facilities.

It is worth noting and debunking the arguments used against the study, as they have been recycled constantly:

- The claim: It doesn't agree with what is obviously happening around the person observing. The reality: Statistics have never had much success in convincing someone who believes something and receives sufficient evidence to support their confirmation bias.

- The claim: The lab is government funded. The reality: The bona fides and independence of the LBNL are topnotch and questioning them indicates the rhetorical or intellectual disposition of the questioner.

- The claim: The study excluded 34 statistical outliers. The reality: Statistical studies of any size do this to eliminate unrepresentative data and 34 exclusions on a sample size of 7,500 is miniscule. This study is accurate and has not been manipulated. . . .

The third major study worth assessing is the Renewable Energy Policy Project's (REPP) 2003 study. While the oldest, it also assessed the largest pool of data prior to 2013, more than 25,000 property transactions in the USA. They looked at every home within five miles (eight kilometers) of ten greater than 10 MW [megawatt] wind developments that came online between 1998 and 2001. They gathered sales data for the control regions near the wind turbines but outside of the five-mile (eight-kilometer) boundary to ensure that they could assess differences accurately. They gathered six years' worth of data covering the years leading up to and following the wind farms' online dates. It is worth noting that while this is by far the largest study with the least statistical adjustment of data, the creator of the study, REPP, is an organization whose public and stated goal is to accelerate the use of renewable energy. As such, while the study design is arguably very good and sample size the largest, it is the only one that might be possible to discount due to source. What REPP found:

- For 8 of the 10 wind projects, property values increased faster inside the five-mile limit than outside of it over the six years.

- For 9 of the 10 wind projects, property values increased faster within the five-mile limit after the wind projects came online than they had before.

- For 9 of the 10 wind projects, property values increased faster within the five-mile limit after the wind projects came online than in the comparable communities.

Not only did this massive study not find negative impacts on real estate values, it found exactly the opposite: *wind turbines have a slight positive impact on real estate values....*

What Is the Evidence That Shows Negative Impacts?

There is a statistically valid, methodologically sound, peer-reviewed study which contradicts the preponderance of evidence above, and is worth detailed assessment as a result. Martin Heintzelman and Carrie Tuttle did a study of 11,331 property transactions over nine years in three counties in northern New York, 461 of which were within three miles of wind turbines. They found that two of the three counties had significant property value decreases while the third had positive indicators. For context, this study is relatively equivalent in terms of organizational respect and depth to [Jennifer L.]

Hinman's study from Illinois State University; credible but not from a world-class organization such as the Berkeley Lab or RICS [Royal Institution of Chartered Surveyors]. A significant failing of the study that makes it difficult to trust compared to other studies is the short time frame of the data for the two counties with negative impacts. Their wind farms became operational in 2008 and 2009, basically in the last year of the data set. The county with positive impacts went live in 2006, in the middle of the data set, providing a much richer analysis space. There are several other significant differences between the two counties that showed negative results and the county with positive results as well. . . .

Despite the largest county with the longest history of wind energy and the most transactions having positive indicators for property values, the authors focused their conclusions dominantly on the negative counties. The authors state in their initial preamble, since revised, that they did not believe it possible that wind turbines didn't negatively affect property values. They found the results they expected, ignoring the significant oddities in their results. This study can only be considered of moderate reliability due to the challenges. . . .

The anecdotes about property value loss represent real people telling the truth as they see it, which is to say, from a limited perspective in both space and time. What they are observing is accurate—lower sales prices than they expected—but their interpretation of the reasons appears to be flawed. However, decisions on policy and legislation must be made on the most robust evidence. The evidence related to property value and wind farms is clear: The only impact that wind farms have is that host properties are worth more after the wind turbines are installed. Nearby properties are unaffected.

> "There is simply no question that IWTs [industrial wind turbines] lower the value of nearby property, and the only legitimate question is, 'how much?,' not 'does it occur?'"

Industrial Wind Turbines Drastically Reduce the Value of Property

Carl V. Phillips

In the following viewpoint, Carl V. Phillips argues that the value of property is lowered if it is near industrial wind turbines (IWTs) and that to deny this requires ignoring both the evidence and the principles of economics. The value of property, he says, is what people are willing to pay for it, and since no one likes living near IWTs, they are not willing to pay as much as they would for comparable property elsewhere. Studies to determine how much the value is reduced may be imperfect, but in his opinion, the fact that some reduction occurs is not open to question. Carl V. Phillips PhD is an epidemiologist and economist. He is a former professor of public health where his contributions to research methodology won numerous awards.

Carl V. Phillips, "Wind Turbines Definitely Lower Local Property Values. The Only Question Is, How Much?," WindTurbineSyndrome.com, February 12, 2014. Copyright © 2014 by Carl V. Phillips. All rights reserved. Reproduced by permission.

As you read, consider the following questions:

1. According to Phillips, what factors cause some people to dislike living near wind turbines?

2. According to Phillips, why are people who do not mind living near wind turbines unwilling to pay as much for property near them as they would for equivalent property elsewhere?

3. According to Phillips, why is the market value of property reduced if the people living there sell because they want to move away from wind turbines?

Large wind generators (IWTs, for "industrial wind turbines") cause health problems for nearby residents, kill birds, and destabilize the power grid. Something those impacts have in common is that it would be *possible* for them to not be the case, and so attempts to deny them represent merely a refusal to acknowledge the overwhelming empirical evidence. That "merely" contrasts with another impact, IWTs lowering local residential property values. Denial of that not only requires ignoring the specific empirical evidence, but requires a suspension of well-established principles of economics.

The value of a piece of real estate is what someone is willing to pay for it. More specifically, in a theoretical perfect market, it is what the person (or family or other entity) who values it second-most would pay for it. This is because whoever values it first-most would have to pay $1 more than that value in order to win the bidding for it. Anything that would cause that person in the second-most position to value the property less, therefore, lowers its value.

Many people are aware of the potential health effects of nearby IWTs, and thus will value a property enormously less if it is near IWTs. For many others, the audible noise or visual impact would lower the value somewhat. If the person who values a property second-most falls into either of these groups, the value of the property will be lower. There is no reason to believe that anyone prefers to have a nearby IWT, so there is no chance that person would like the property more and thus increase the value. (Note that this analysis does not consider the net change in the value of a property with income from IWTs that are actually on the property. For such properties, there will still be a decrease in value from the proximity but might be a net increase because the income more than makes up for this.)

Moreover, even someone who does not personally worry about the health risk or find the aesthetic impacts objectionable will know that others do. Thus, he will know that the potential resale value of the property is lower, and since that contributes to the value, this will tend to push down the value for even those who do not mind living near the IWTs.

Thus, there is simply no question that IWTs lower the value of nearby property, and the only legitimate question is, "how much?," not "does it occur?" Anyone who insists that there is no reduction in value is trafficking in nonsense that is actually one step worse than the nonsense that there are no health impacts, in that it denies both the evidence and the irrefutable logic.

Real Loss of Value

Of course, in reality, markets do not function exactly like the theoretical simplification, but the same principle applies in the real world with only a bit of additional complication. The sale of a property does not attract the attention of everyone who might want to bid, and so the second-highest valuation is not based on every possible buyer, but only on those who are in the market at the particular time. But this changes nothing. More significantly, the market is not a perfect auction, so the highest offer (which determines the market value of the property) does not consist literally of someone outbidding the second-highest by $1, but rather some guesswork about what

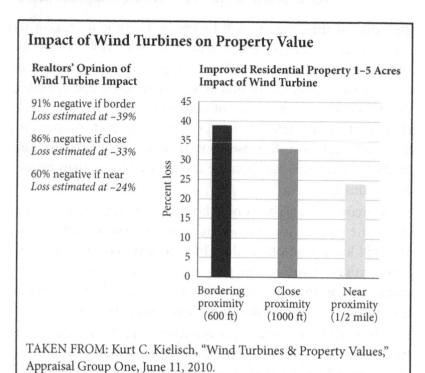

Impact of Wind Turbines on Property Value

Realtors' Opinion of Wind Turbine Impact

91% negative if border
Loss estimated at –39%

86% negative if close
Loss estimated at –33%

60% negative if near
Loss estimated at –24%

Improved Residential Property 1–5 Acres Impact of Wind Turbine

Percent loss (y-axis: 0, 5, 10, 15, 20, 25, 30, 35, 40, 45)

Bordering proximity (600 ft)
Close proximity (1000 ft)
Near proximity (1/2 mile)

TAKEN FROM: Kurt C. Kielisch, "Wind Turbines & Property Values," Appraisal Group One, June 11, 2010.

bid is enough to convince the seller that no better offer is available. But this offer will be no higher than the potential buyer's value for the property, which will be lowered by the factors noted above, and the guesses about alternative offers will be pushed downward by those factors also. Thus the exact real-world results may not be as predictable as the theoretical case, but the fact that there is a reduction in value is unchanged.

Finally, the person/family who values a property the most is almost always, by far, the one who is living there. This is why very few sales result from an interested buyer making an offer for a property that is not actively for sale. So when residents suffer problems from nearby IWTs that make them want to move, the market value is dramatically reduced because the bidding for the property no longer includes the person who previously placed the highest value on it. Even worse than this impact on the market value, the benefits from that piece of land to overall human happiness—because it no longer provides net benefits to those who valued it the most—is reduced even more.

Empirical studies are required to determine *how much* property values are decreased near IWTs, and that magnitude might affect policy decisions and certainly affects cost-benefit analyses. The methods for doing such studies are highly imperfect; hence, there is room to criticize the estimated magnitude.

One thing we know for sure is that any study or assertion that insists there is no impact is wrong.

Periodical and Internet Sources Bibliography

The following articles have been selected to supplement the diverse views presented in this chapter.

Trevor Brown — "Report: Wyo. Wind Could Compete with Natural Gas," *Wyoming Tribune-Eagle* (Cheyenne, WY), September 1, 2013.

Emma G. Fitzsimmons — "Wind Energy Company to Pay $1 Million in Bird Deaths," *New York Times*, November 22, 2013.

Dan Frosch — "A Struggle to Balance Wind Energy with Wildlife," *New York Times*, December 16, 2013.

Laura Gaddy — "Winds of Change: Alternative Energy Source Planned for Shinbone Ridge," *Anniston Star* (Anniston, AL), July 18, 2013.

Tim McDonnell — "Top 4 Reasons the US Still Doesn't Have a Single Offshore Wind Turbine," *Mother Jones*, February 28, 2013.

Elliott Negin — "Wind Energy Threat to Birds Is Overblown," *Huffington Post*, November 22, 2013.

Josh O'Kane — "Can Wind Power Cut Northern Dependence on Diesel?," *Globe and Mail* (Toronto, Canada), April 4, 2014.

Gene Russo — "Renewable Energy: Wind Power Tests the Waters," *Nature*, September 24, 2014.

Katharine Q. Seelye — "Koch Brother Wages 12-Year Fight Over Wind Farm," *New York Times*, October 22, 2013.

Kate Sheppard — "Wind Power Has Cut U.S. Carbon Dioxide Emissions by 4.4 Percent: Report," *Huffington Post*, April 4, 2014.

OPPOSING
VIEWPOINTS®
SERIES

CHAPTER 3

Is Utility-Scale Solar Power a Practical Alternative Energy Source?

Chapter Preface

On April 25, 1954, Bell Laboratories announced that researchers had developed the first photovoltaic cells capable of converting solar energy to a useful amount of electricity. The invention was demonstrated at a meeting of the National Academy of Sciences, causing the *New York Times* to declare that it might mark "the beginning of a new era, eventually leading to the realization of one of mankind's most cherished dreams—the harnessing of the almost limitless energy of the sun for the uses of civilization."

Solar energy has been used since ancient times for heating by means of direct exposure to sunlight, and in the late nineteenth and early twentieth centuries, sun-power generators that heated water to produce steam were developed. In the September 30, 1911, issue of *Scientific American*, such a generator was described. "The future development of solar power has no limit," wrote author Frank Shuman. "Where great natural water powers exist the sun cannot compete; but sun-power generators will, in the near future, displace all other forms of mechanical power over at least 10 percent of the earth's land surface; and in the far distant future, natural fuels having been exhausted, it will remain as the only means of existence of the human race."

In the modern world, however, electricity has supplanted steam power, and the generation of electric power from sunlight does not always involve heat. In photovoltaic systems, solar radiation energizes electrons in a semiconductor such as silicon to generate electricity. The first practical use of photovoltaic cells was as the power source for America's first satellite, Vanguard, in 1958. Solar power continued to be used in space, where cost was not a factor, throughout the 1960s, but the cells were then too expensive for commercial use on land. Not until the 1970s did the price drop enough for them to be used where electricity was needed far from power lines, for example, on offshore oil rigs. Since then, photovoltaic technology has progressed to the point where solar panels are readily available for powering homes and businesses.

Utility-scale solar power—electricity fed to power lines instead of being used off grid—took longer to develop. In 1982 the first megawatt-scale photovoltaic power station went online. In that same year, a demonstration solar-thermal system commenced operation. Solar-thermal power plants use heat from the sun to produce steam, which drives turbines to produce electricity. The heat is concentrated by mirrors called heliostats that track the sun and focus it on a central receiver atop a tower. Such installations can generate electricity less expensively than photovoltaic plants and on a larger scale; moreover, the energy they produce can be stored in the form of molten salt so that steam can be produced even when the sun is not shining.

The ultimate use of photovoltaic power—its generation in space where the sun always shines with no interference from an atmosphere—was first proposed back in 1968. Space-based solar power received a good deal of attention during the 1970s but was deemed too expensive to be feasible because of the high cost of launching components into space. Some experts still believe space-based power generation is a feasible way of meeting Earth's growing need for electricity. In April of 2014, the first serious plan for actual generation of space-based solar power was announced by Japan.

This chapter discusses utility-scale solar power as a practical alternative energy source.

> "The steep drop in photovoltaic panel costs over the last decade will continue, meaning true cost parity for solar—compared to natural gas or coal—can be achieved in the next few years."

The Cost of Utility-Scale Solar Power Is Dropping

Dave Levitan

In the following viewpoint, Dave Levitan reports that the cost of building utility-scale solar power plants is dropping, but the future of such plants is uncertain because distributed solar power, or power that comes from panels on individual buildings, may prove dominant. Furthermore, he contends, it is not known whether federal subsidies for the utility-scale solar market will continue. It may become difficult for solar industry officials to find purchasers for their power. Since some states are requiring utilities to store power, solar facilities that can provide energy storage are likely to have an advantage. Levitan is a Philadelphia-based journalist who writes about energy, the environment, and health.

Dave Levitan, "For Utility-Scale Solar Industry, Key Questions About the Future," *Environment 360*, November 21, 2013. Copyright © 2013 by Dave Levitan. All rights reserved. Reproduced by permission.

As you read, consider the following questions:

1. According to Levitan, what two factors have caused the recent expansion of utility-scale solar power?

2. According to a US Department of Energy estimate, how many megawatts of utility-scale solar power could be integrated into the power supply by 2030?

3. What percentage of US electrical capacity did utility-scale solar power account for at the end of 2012, according to the viewpoint?

In the United States today [2013], large "utility-scale" solar power projects account for more than 4,700 megawatts of electricity-generating capacity. Another 27,000 megawatts of large-scale solar are under development, which means that the industrial-solar sector is on its way to providing enough electricity for more than 5 million homes.

These are impressive numbers, but the question now is: Will this growth continue? Much of the expansion of utility-scale solar power—which consists of large, ground-mounted arrays of photovoltaic [PV] panels or another technology called concentrating solar power—has been due to two factors: state renewable energy portfolio standards that require utilities to produce a certain amount of green energy, and federal tax credits set to be sharply reduced at the end of 2016.

As the overall solar industry pushes past 10,000 megawatts of installed power by the end of the year—including PV panels on the roofs of homes and businesses—some states will soon begin to achieve renewable energy targets mandated by state portfolio standards, which could dampen demand for utility-scale solar projects. Given that and the uncertainty over federal tax credits, will the large solar plants starting to dot the U.S. Southwest and elsewhere keep cropping up? Or will utility-scale solar fizzle out even as the need to push all forms of renewable energy forward becomes more urgent?

Utility-Scale vs. Distributed Solar Power

Some renewable energy experts say the future of utility-scale solar is far from assured, in part because they believe distributed solar—meaning panels on individual buildings—will become increasingly dominant as the price of PV panels continues to fall.

Other analysts say that both distributed solar and utility-scale solar will play an important role in U.S. electricity generation. Today, solar power is just one percent of the total installed electricity capacity in the U.S. But experts believe that several trends could solidify the position of industrial-scale solar going forward. The first is the rapidly declining cost and increasing efficiency of photovoltaic and other solar technologies. The second is the likelihood that state and federal policies—including renewable energy portfolio standard (RPS) mandates, which now exist in 29 states and the District of Columbia, and a major federal tax incentive—will be extended or expanded.

In addition, the federal government has big plans for utility-scale solar. The U.S. Department of Energy's SunShot initiative, an effort to bring the cost of solar down, projects a scenario where costs continue to drop dramatically and 329,000 megawatts of solar power are integrated into the power supply by 2030, representing 13.8 percent of total electricity demand in the U.S. Of that, the Department of Energy estimates 209,000 megawatts, or almost two-thirds, could be utility-scale solar if prices for solar technology continue to fall.

"Ultimately the real beauty of solar is that every building, every car park is covered," says Dan Kammen, a professor of energy at the University of California, Berkeley. "So in the decades ahead, we'll go to more and more distributed, but to enable the transition, I think we will see more of these bigger facilities still being installed."

According to Cory Honeyman, a solar analyst at GTM Research, utility-scale photovoltaics alone accounted for only 0.25 percent of the total U.S. electricity capacity at the end of 2012. By the end of 2016, he says, that number will jump to 1.6 percent, more than a 500 percent increase.

But building big solar is tough—projects face significant regulatory hurdles—and expensive. Large solar plants like Ivanpah, Solana, and the California Valley Solar Ranch are getting built in a few states because it is financially feasible based on existing policies. "Utility companies don't tend to do these things voluntarily," says Martin Pasqualetti, a professor and expert on energy policy at Arizona State University in Tempe.

Renewable Energy Mandates

Today, utility companies generally buy the power from big solar plants to fulfill RPS mandates. California, for example, is requiring that 33 percent of the state's electricity needs come from renewables by 2020. A utility can take a big chunk out of its RPS mandate by buying all the power produced at a 100-megawatt plant, and they're doing so at numerous installations in the sunny parts of the country, including California, Nevada, and Arizona.

The utilities are buying up that power to avoid substantial financial penalties. "These RPS standards with penalties for non-compliance created this demand," Honeyman says.

Because the utilities have an incentive to buy the power, the developers of the solar plants can secure financing to build them. The high-profile, 377-megawatt Ivanpah plant—ramping up to full capacity in California's Mojave Desert right now—cost $2.2 billion, and other big projects are similarly expensive. Major loans from the Department of Energy help many of them pay those lofty costs. The other policy helping the projects along is the federal investment tax credit, or ITC, which offers a 30 percent credit for facilities that come online by the end of 2016. But what happens if the tax credits are not extended and RPS mandates are fulfilled—and potentially not extended or amended?

Those policy shifts are the backdrop for the fact that the impressive pipeline of projects under construction or development is starting to run out of steam. Honeyman, of GTM Research, says that the slowdown is happening faster than anticipated. Some of the largest projects listed by the Solar Energy Industries Association (SEIA) . . . have no entry under "electricity purchaser." A project that can't promise an opening date before 2017—when tax credits are scheduled to drop to 10 percent—may be struggling to find a purchaser for its electricity.

Rooftop solar faces fewer uncertainties and is expanding rapidly, with 488 megawatts installed in 2012, 62 percent more than the previous year. Individual incentives at the state and federal level, along with innovative solar leasing models where a building or house owner pays nothing up front, are pushing rooftop solar along just fine. But utilities generally aren't enthusiastic about such "distributed generation," since they make no money off those sources of power.

"Ultimately we're likely to see solar as very distributed, because we might as well take advantage of our urban landscape and cover our built surfaces," says Kammen, who has frequently testified to Congress on renewable energy issues. "But utilities are much more comfortable with large, central station power plants, and they demonstrate again and again that they're not really that well positioned . . . for distributed solar."

Many utilities themselves are cautious. In California, San Diego Gas & Electric has signed renewable energy contracts totaling around 1,750 megawatts of power generation since

US Deployment and Cost for Solar PV Modules 2008–2012

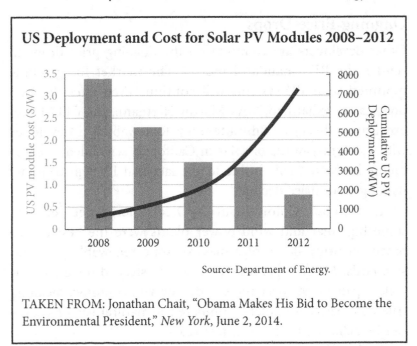

Source: Department of Energy.

TAKEN FROM: Jonathan Chait, "Obama Makes His Bid to Become the Environmental President," *New York*, June 2, 2014.

2011, but a spokesperson for the utility says only that it will "meet or exceed" the 2020 RPS mandate and that further renewables procurement may focus more on energy efficiency efforts, energy storage, or "more traditional types of generation."

But developers of utility-scale solar say they aren't particularly worried, citing both dropping costs of solar and optimism that state and federal incentives will continue. "Renewable portfolio standards have always been the biggest driver of utility-scale solar development, and we're cautiously optimistic we will see these standards continue to be raised across the country," says Steve Schooff, the director of communications for California-based Sempra U.S. Gas & Power, a developer with more than 300 megawatts of utility-scale solar in operation and hundreds more in development. He adds that some states such as Nevada are looking into early retirement of coal plants, with solar among the replacement technologies.

Ongoing Price Drops

Other developers are counting on the ongoing price drops to render the RPS mandates moot. "The market for ground-mounted solar PV systems will continue even after the RPS policies are exhausted," says Martin Hermann, the CEO [chief executive officer] of 8minutenergy Renewables, a developer with 2,000 megawatts of solar in California scheduled to come online by 2016. "This is due to the fact that PV will continue its long-term price decline."

In October, Colorado utility Xcel Energy decided that some big solar and wind power plants were the best choice based on price alone, regardless of state renewable portfolio standards. Many experts agree that the steep drop in photovoltaic panel costs over the last decade will continue, meaning true cost parity for solar—compared to natural gas or coal—can be achieved in the next few years.

Stefan Reichelstein, a professor at Stanford University, says cost parity with natural gas is more likely to arrive in a decade or so. Thus, the industry will make an argument that "extending the federal subsidies for a number of years beyond 2016 will be essential in order to preserve the pace of new installations," he says. Jared Blanton, a spokesperson for Ivanpah codeveloper BrightSource Energy, says even a tweak of that federal tax credit to allow projects to simply "commence construction" rather than enter into service by 2016 would boost the utility-scale solar market.

One recently approved California policy will also help support the utility-scale solar industry. The nation's first-ever energy-storage mandate, requiring utilities to purchase 1,325 megawatts of energy storage by 2020, is a natural fit for big solar plants. Facilities that use concentrating solar power—which involves mirrors focusing light on a pipe or central tower to create power-generating steam—can incorporate big storage solutions relatively seamlessly. Abengoa's Solana plant in the Arizona desert features molten salt storage that allows the plant to feed power to the grid for six hours after the sun goes down. Other companies, particularly in California, will likely follow suit.

"Big facilities make sense as long as they're integrating storage," Kammen says, adding that a major research push into storage—focused on everything from batteries to compressed air systems—could play an important role in helping utility-scale solar expand.

And should the federal government ever put a price on carbon, utility-scale solar will become ever more competitive, some experts contend. Says Arizona State University's Pasqualetti, "Eventually it will be so obviously the option, both economically and environmentally, that there will be no question that we should be moving more solidly into a solar future."

| "*To wean California off fossil fuels, California mandates the existence of fossil fuel–powered backup generators because the solar power isn't reliable enough.*"

Utility-Scale Solar Power Is Uneconomical and Unreliable

Mark Landsbaum

In the following viewpoint, Mark Landsbaum argues that industrial-scale solar power is not as friendly to the environment as is claimed, since it involves covering millions of acres of desert with solar panels that kill or endanger wildlife with heat generation, light reflection, vibration, dust, and noise. He also points out that its true cost is hidden because much of it is paid by taxpayers through tax credits and other subsidies to the solar power industry, as well as through higher utility bills for consumers, and it does not create many jobs. Furthermore, he says, industrial-scale solar power is so unreliable that fossil fuel backup generators are required. Landsbaum is a staff columnist at the Orange County Register, *a California newspaper.*

Mark Landsbaum, "Skeptical of Solar Salvation," *Orange County Register*, August 21, 2013. Copyright © 2013 by Orange County Register. All rights reserved. Reproduced by permission.

As you read, consider the following questions:

1. According to the viewpoint, how much public land has the Obama administration designated for utility-scale solar facilities?

2. Why do environmentalists and Native Americans object to the large-scale solar power plants in California?

3. According to Landsbaum, at what percentage do solar power plants operate?

The future, we are assured, is in solar energy. It is clean, environmentally friendly, economical, ubiquitous, renewable with every sunrise and as reliable as sunshine itself.

They mean well. Or maybe they don't. Either way, you would be prudent to be skeptical.

Before we count the ways we are fleeced by the promise of solar salvation, let's assess the state of things.

The [Barack] Obama administration has designated up to 445 square miles of public land for utility-scale solar facilities, the *Los Angeles Times* reported. This comes on top of 17 solar facilities already awarded permits, and 78 more in various stages of approval.

California Gov. Jerry Brown, to whom nothing green brings offense, is party to the plan to cover the desert with solar panels. Brown even has threatened to "crush" solar opponents, because "nothing's gonna stop me." The governor seems always willing to work for your best interest, and if you don't think so, he'll "crush" you to prove it.

With Washington and Sacramento so obviously committed, this must be a good thing, right?

Perhaps the best argument in favor of relying on sunshine to run your computer and keep the house lights on is it is nonpolluting.

True, solar panels spew no toxic emissions. But how environmentally friendly are they? Thousands of garage door–size solar panels, side by side, on millions of acres, capturing heat to transfer to skyscraper-sized water towers to create steam to generate electricity.

"[I]n the name of saving the planet, we're casting aside 30 or 40 years of environmental law," Christine Hersey, a solar analyst at Wedbush Securities, lamented to the *Desert Sun* newspaper in Palm Springs.

Numerous large-scale solar plants in Riverside and Imperial Counties alarmed "environmentalists, Native Americans and others . . . saying it's running roughshod over threatened plant and animal species," the newspaper reported last year [2012]. Critics worried irreparable damage would be done to historic, prehistoric and culturally important sites.

Well, at least the economics pencil out. Don't they?

Not exactly.

Hidden Costs

Let's start with hidden costs. Whether panels on your roof top, or acres of panels spread over the desert, none cost what the buyer pays. Real costs are masked by taxpayer and ratepayer subsidies. How many homeowners would pony up the full cost of producing and peddling rooftop panels? Likewise, companies that develop acres of solar farms to generate electricity couldn't make a profit if they paid full cost.

A peek behind the solar curtain reveals how it is made "affordable." Taxpayers pay a huge chunk of costs long before they flip the light switch. More than a third of the cost of construction of a $141 million Nevada solar facility was paid for with $42 million in federal tax credits and $12 million in state tax rebates.

"The solar industry as we see it today isn't likely to exist without subsidies," observes Brian McGraw of the Competitive Enterprise Institute.

Ratepayers also subsidize the solar game in higher utility bills.

It may be difficult to put a price on environmental havoc wracked by the Ivanpah solar project in the Mojave Desert that killed desert tortoises and endangered other indigenous critters with heat generation, light reflection, vibration, dust and noise. But the $2 billion project's capital costs run three times more expensive than natural gas or coal, according to the National Center for Policy Analysis, which quotes the state Public Utilities Commission's conclusion that "as a result," electricity consumers will see their bills increase up to 50 percent for renewable energy.

"We need to remember that at some point, the [solar] industry will have to survive without ratepayer subsidies," said Stefanie Brand, director of the Division of Rate Counsel [of the State of New Jersey] in testimony before the [New Jersey] Senate Environment and Energy Committee. "The idea was that ratepayers would help jump-start the market, not sustain it forever."

In the current lingua franca, how "*sustainable*" is an unprofitable industry requiring subsidies at both ends of the chain of production?

At least these subsidies reduce costs to create solar power, right? Not exactly.

The Electric Power Research Institute calculates a 1,000 megawatt conventional coal-fired plant costs about $2.8 billion to build, compared with a solar plant of similar output at $6.6 billion. Not only is solar more expensive, but coal plants operate at 90 percent capacity compared to only 30 percent for solar. To produce the same output, the solar facility would have to increase in size, and its cost would balloon to $20 billion.

By Nature Unreliable

Even though solar energy is awfully costly and not quite as eco-friendly, at least it's ubiquitous. After all, the sun shines every day. Right? Sort of.

Solar, like wind power, is *by nature unreliable*, points out Daniel Kish, senior vice president at the Institute for Energy Research. The sun shines and the wind blows intermittently, therefore unreliably.

Don't take his word for it. Even the state of California, that beacon of sun power, acknowledged this drawback this year when "regulators forced utilities to prop up a gas plant facing closure," wrote the Reason Foundation's Adam Peshek. "Their reasoning: as the state continues to scale up renewable energy, affordable fossil fuels need to be there as backup."

Let that sink in. To wean California off fossil fuels, California mandates the existence of fossil fuel–powered backup generators because the solar power isn't reliable enough. It's the worst of both worlds: solar's exorbitant costs and fossil fuel's greenhouse gas emissions (although yours truly finds the first considerably more offensive than the latter).

Nevertheless, more solar generating plants are ahead, as the numbers show and projections predict. At least for now.

At least solar farms as far as the eye can see should boost local economies, right? Didn't President Barack Obama promise millions of green jobs from just such stuff?

A proposed $2.7 billion solar power plant 230 miles northeast of Los Angeles promised a job bonanza and heaps of taxes for Inyo County government. "But upon closer inspection," the *Los Angeles Times* reported, "the picture didn't seem so rosy."

The revenue boost instead would be "a fraction of the customary amount" because solar projects get tax exemptions to encourage their construction. Fewer than 10 local workers would get permanent jobs, a consultant told the county, and local residents would get only 5 percent of the construction jobs. There also would be unreimbursed costs, such as up to $12 million to upgrade a road to the new plant. Once the solar plant comes online, the county estimates it would cost taxpayers almost another $2 million a year to provide public safety and other services.

"Riverside and San Bernardino, have made similar discoveries," the *[Los Angeles] Times* reported.

"[W]here are the benefits to the county?" asked Gerry Newcombe, San Bernardino County public works director.

San Bernardino County supervisor John Benoit complained, "The solar companies are the beneficiaries of huge government loans, tax credits and, most critically for me, property tax exemptions, at the expense of taxpayers."

Here we have the explanation of what really is going on in the mad rush to adopt uneconomical, impractical and unreliable solar power. There are great benefits to be had—just not by the people paying the bills.

> "As we enter the evaluation period of significant investments in solar energy, the industry is closely watching SolarReserve's Crescent Dunes project."

New Technology May Make Utility-Scale Solar Power More Cost-Efficient

Noreen Moustafa

In the following viewpoint, Noreen Moustafa reports on the Crescent Dunes Solar Energy Project, a large industrial-scale solar energy facility under construction in Nevada that employs technology new to the United States. Although solar power is presently more expensive than other energy sources, this new technology that converts the sun's rays to energy and then stores the power for future use is expected to make it less so. The Crescent Dunes facility is being developed with support from the federal government as well as from private investors, and it is too soon to know whether the investment will pay off. Supporters, however, believe the project may provide a model for solar energy providers. Moustafa is a producer at the television news channel Al Jazeera America.

Noreen Moustafa, "Sustainability of Solar Energy at a Crossroads," Al Jazeera America, January 22, 2014. Copyright © 2014 by Al Jazeera America. All rights reserved. Reproduced by permission.

As you read, consider the following questions:

1. According to the viewpoint, what new technology for generating solar power is used in the Crescent Dunes Solar Energy Project?

2. According to the US Department of Energy, how much will the Crescent Dunes project reduce the release of carbon dioxide annually?

3. To how many homes will Crescent Dunes be able to provide power?

As you approach the dusty Nevada town of Tonopah on a desolate two-lane highway, you can't miss the giant tower rising up on the horizon. There is a red light on top that flashes like a beacon, signaling to all passing traffic that this is not a mirage or an environmentalist's desert fever dream.

The tower is part of the Crescent Dunes Solar Energy Project, a sustainable solar field built about 200 miles north of Las Vegas by the California-based company SolarReserve. It's the first of its kind in the U.S.—a 24/7 energy plant that uses giant mirrors and molten salt to capture the sun's rays, convert them to energy and store that energy until power is needed.

The scale of the project is striking—both visually and by the numbers. According to the Department of Energy [DOE], this facility alone will reduce the release of nearly 280,000 metric tons of carbon dioxide annually—"equivalent to the emissions of more than 50,000 vehicles." The Crescent Dunes project is still under construction, with 8,500 tracking mirrors, or heliostats, assembled so far on a 1,500-acre field.

The development of such a large project required a confluence of support from private and public investment, most notably that of the federal government, which under President Barack Obama drastically increased its commitment to clean energy. In September 2011, the Department of Energy gave

SolarReserve a $737 million loan guarantee for a 110-megawatt solar-power tower, which it also allowed to be built on federal land.

The price for solar power is still higher than what utility companies pay for energy from traditional sources, but utilities have increasing incentives to diversify their energy portfolios. Thirty states, including big markets like California, are now required by their own laws to buy a significant portion of their energy from renewable resources such as solar, and another seven states have set more voluntary goals. In California, 33 percent of energy must come from renewable sources by 2020.

Before even contributing power back to the grid, SolarReserve secured a 25-year power purchase agreement with Nevada's utility company, NV Energy, which is aiming for 25 percent renewable energy by 2025. This will, of course, assist in the repayment of the loan, but it also helps promote solar power long term.

Even with many states on pace to match California's and Nevada's requirements, trends in the industry show that the solar building boom—kicked off by the Obama administration nearly five years ago when the president signed a $787 billion economic stimulus package with major clean energy incentives—may actually soon be over.

An Open Question

The question that remains is whether the investment will lead to future purchases of solar power. Prices for natural gas continue to plummet, making it an appealing alternative for utility companies, even though natural gas is not considered as clean as solar power. As bottom lines are examined, utilities may be more swayed by cost than impact.

As a country, the U.S. had made progress in reducing carbon emissions by 12 percent since 2008. However, now that

What Is a Power Tower?

A power tower converts sunshine into clean electricity for the world's electricity grids. The technology utilizes many large, sun-tracking mirrors (heliostats) to focus sunlight on a receiver at the top of a tower. A heat transfer fluid heated in the receiver is used to generate steam, which, in turn, is used in a conventional turbine generator to produce electricity. Early power towers . . . utilized steam as the heat transfer fluid; current designs . . . utilize molten nitrate salt because of its superior heat transfer and energy storage capabilities.

Solar power towers . . . are unique among solar electric technologies in their ability to efficiently store solar energy and dispatch electricity to the grid when needed—even at night or during cloudy weather. A single 100-megawatt power tower with 12 hours of storage needs only 1000 acres of otherwise nonproductive land to supply enough electricity for 50,000 homes.

"Solar Power Towers Deliver Energy Solutions,"
Waste Isolation Pilot Plant (WIPP),
US Department of Energy, 2014.

DOE loan guarantees have expired, those gains could easily be lost as the solar subsidies fade and shale gas prices plummet. Without price parity—which is common in European markets—we may not be able to maintain the progress we've made beyond the mandated benchmarks.

Tonopah's town manager, James Eason, agrees that there has to be a mix of economic and environmental benefits, but believes in solar as a long-term solution. "If people's energy prices stay relatively flat, I think they'll be happy," Eason told *TechKnow* [a TV program on Al Jazeera America].

"We know solar is the more expensive power," he said. "But over time there is not a market on rays of the sun. The one thing that's a little bit different about this project is that their raw material—it's not subject to an Enron, or somebody like that, that is manipulating the fuel price."

In markets like India and Africa, solar energy is more affordable than diesel-based energy production. As we enter the evaluation period of significant investments in solar energy, the industry is closely watching SolarReserve's Crescent Dunes project—which is just months away from being able to provide power to 70,000 Nevada homes. It's the first commercial application of molten-salt technology in the U.S., and when construction is done, it will be the largest molten-salt power tower in the world. It could present a new—and more cost-efficient—model for solar energy providers, and by one estimate would raise rates by only about 1 percent.

SolarReserve CEO [chief executive officer] Kevin Smith predicts that this facility will leapfrog the U.S. into a leadership position in terms of solar technology, and that in years to come, the energy market will reflect that—especially if the federal and state governments continue to make it a priority.

"We shouldn't just let the markets decide," Smith said. "This is critical to life. It's critical to advancement of society. It's critical to everything that we do. And so there's every reason in the world for government to be involved in our energy future, to make sure that we're doing the right things."

| "The use of solar power cannot be increased without also increasing existing frequency regulation services."

Solar Power May Be Difficult to Integrate with Existing Power Networks

Ker Than

In the following viewpoint, Ker Than explains that harnessing solar energy is not the only technological problem that would have to be solved for utility-scale solar power to provide more than a small percentage of the nation's power. It is necessary to keep power generation and total power load in balance. He explains this can be done with existing power sources because they can be controlled, but solar power is inconsistent, as rapidly moving clouds can affect the amount of energy generated from moment to moment. To overcome this, he says, frequency regulation generators are used, but these are expensive and to have too many of these would increase the cost of solar power. Therefore, Than concludes, new technologies for handling power surges are being investigated. Than is a contributor to the Inside Science News Service (ISNS).

Ker Than, "Harnessing Sun's Energy Presents Challenges to Existing Power Networks," Inside Science, June 6, 2013. Copyright © 2013 American Institute of Physics. All rights reserved. Used with permission.

As you read, consider the following questions:

1. According to the viewpoint, what do frequency regulation generators do to compensate for inconsistency in the output of solar power cells?

2. According to estimates by experts, what percentage of US power could be supplied by utility-scale solar power without increasing the number of frequency regulation generators now in use?

3. What is "islanding," and why must it be prevented, according to the viewpoint?

One hour's worth of global sunlight would be enough to power the world's energy requirements for an entire year. But even if humankind can someday harness solar power to meet global energy needs, there is another problem engineers will have to tackle: integrating solar power with existing electrical networks.

In a new review of existing research, published online in the *Journal of Renewable and Sustainable Energy*, scientists warn that this latter challenge will not be easy because solar cells—also known as photovoltaic, or PV, cells—have numerous negative impacts on current systems used to distribute electrical power.

For example, one potential problem is keeping power systems balanced as PV cells enter the existing network so that the total amount of electricity generated is always equal to the amount of electricity used by the network, explained study coauthor Mohamed Elnozahy, an electrical and computer engineer at Canada's University of Waterloo.

If these two factors—total power generation and total load—are not kept balanced at all times, "severe frequency and voltage problems would occur," Elnozahy said.

"Right now, we don't face this power balance problem, as conventional generators are controllable to a great extent."

Fickle Sunlight

Solar power, on the other hand, is much more inconsistent. The amount of power generated by PV cells can change dramatically in response to unpredictable environmental factors such as cloud cover and temperature. Fast-moving clouds, for example, can reduce the electrical output of PV systems by up to 50 percent within a few seconds.

To compensate for solar power fluctuations, engineers currently incorporate fast but relatively expensive generators that perform frequency regulation services. These generators inject extra power into networks when fluctuations in PV output cause the generated electricity to dip below the desired frequency of 60 hertz.

The use of solar power cannot be increased without also increasing existing frequency regulation services, Elnozahy said. "This will increase the cost of solar electricity, which is already much higher than other sources," he said.

Some experts predict that without increasing the number of frequency regulation generators in use, solar power won't be able to supply more than 5 percent of our current power demands.

One possible remedy to this problem is being pursued by Elnozahy and Magdy Salama, a professor of electrical engineering at the University of Waterloo and a coauthor of the new paper.

Their solution involves developing a new "bilayer architecture" for the distribution of solar power that is composed of three basic components: an alternating current, or AC, layer, which covers the existing electrical grid, except for solar power; a direct current, or DC layer, that is dedicated to collecting solar electricity; and a "controlled inverter interface" that controls the power flow between the two layers.

The architecture will be challenging to adopt but "will ensure that solar electricity is completely decoupled from AC networks," Elnozahy explained.

New Ways of Connecting Mini-Grids

Grid interconnection of renewable energy systems, including mini-grids, is a rapidly evolving landscape. New technologies including advanced integrated relays, synchrophasors, new networking devices, prepaid energy metering systems, and super-efficient loads keep entering the market, and policy makers and regulators struggle to keep up with the changes.

As one example of an emerging technology application for mini-grids, inexpensive data transmission over mobile phone networks or by satellite can be used for Internet-based monitoring and control of mini-grids, including dispatch. . . . This wireless technology is a low-cost alternative to fiber optic lines or leased phone lines and would work anywhere there is a mobile phone signal or where a satellite dish can be deployed. . . .

On the policy side, power purchase agreements for renewable energy SPPs [small power producers] have conventionally been 'must take' contracts where the utility must compensate the SPP for all energy exported to the grid at all times. As renewable energy penetration increases, and policy makers continue to strive for even more grid-tied renewables, contracts that allow for either dispatchable renewable generation and/or curtailment on a signal from the utility for a certain number of hours per year will be useful tools for bringing more renewable capacity online without threatening grid stability or having to dump power.

Chris Greacen, Richard Engel, and Thomas Quetchenbach,
"A Guidebook on Grid Interconnection and Islanded Operation
of Mini-Grid Power Systems Up to 200 kW," Lawrence Berkeley
National Laboratory and Schatz Energy Research Center,
April 2013.

As a result, power surges in the solar electricity, or DC, network will not affect the existing power grid.

Problems Solved?

Willett Kempton, a professor in the College of Earth, Ocean, and Environment at the University of Delaware who was not involved in the study, acknowledged that many of the challenges to solar power implementation highlighted by the review paper are real, but notes that some of them already have solutions or are relatively simple to solve.

For example, another problem highlighted in the paper is "islanding," which refers to the condition in which a power generator continues to produce electricity even after the electric grid has been shut down. Islanding is very hazardous to utility workers attempting to restore power and to equipment. As a result, utility companies prohibit equipment that does not prevent islanding.

Elnozahy and Salama argue that while techniques exist to detect islanding in PV systems, many of them have "nondetection zones"—that is, certain voltage and power values that fail to trigger a timely response. Furthermore, these techniques would drive up the overall cost of integrating solar and electrical networks.

Kempton disagreed. "This is a solved problem," he said. "I am working now with an inverter that is totally reliable in detecting islanding . . . and has no nondetection zones."

Kempton is very optimistic about the future of renewable energy, including solar power. In a study published in the *Journal of Power Sources*, he and his team predicted that a combination of wind power, solar power, and improved batteries and fuel cells could fully power a large electrical grid 99.9 percent of the time by 2030 at costs comparable to today's electricity expenses.

Elnozahy notes that the challenges he highlights in the paper are not unique to solar power.

"Wind power suffers similar problems," he said. "However, solar power is highly dependent on atmospheric conditions and thus, these problems are more significant for solar."

| "Experts say investments in large-scale solar power projects could transform a continent faced with fast-rising populations and increasing demand for energy to support its economic growth."

Bright Sun, Bright Future: Can Africa Unlock Its Solar Potential?

Teo Kermeliotis

In the following viewpoint, Teo Kermeliotis reports on the current status of industrial-scale power generation in Africa. One very large solar photovoltaic (PV) plant is being built in Africa with support from Google, and other solar programs are under way in a number of African countries. Nevertheless, only a small percentage of Africa's power comes from solar energy, and insufficient awareness of its feasibility, problems with financing, and lack of political commitment are preventing the rapid growth that is needed. Kermeliotis is an online journalist specializing in international affairs, financial news, and human rights issues.

Teo Kermeliotis, "Bright Sun, Bright Future: Can Africa Unlock Its Solar Potential?," From CNN.com, August 29 © 2013 Cable News Network, Inc. All rights reserved. Used by permission and protected by the Copyright Laws of the United States. The printing, copying, redistribution, or retransmission of this Content without express written permission is prohibited.

As you read, consider the following questions:

1. According to the author, what country has the world's highest growth in renewable energy investment?

2. According to the International Energy Agency, what percentage of Africa's power generation in 2009 was accounted for by coal, oil, and gas?

3. According to the United Nations Environment Programme (UNEP), what will be the result if current trends in power generation are not reversed?

Which country boasts the world's fastest-growing clean energy investment? Germany? No. United States? Think again.

Jumping from a few hundred million dollars to $5.7 billion, South Africa recorded last year [2012] the world's highest growth in renewable energy investment, according to the U.N. [United Nations] Environment Programme (UNEP).

The spectacular surge, led largely by investments in solar power projects, comes as South Africa moves to reduce its dependency on coal, which accounts for around 86% of its energy. To achieve that, the country has set the ambitious target of generating 18 gigawatts (GW) of clean energy by 2030.

As a result, a series of investments have trickled into the country, including Google's first foray into Africa's solar power market. The Internet giant, which has spent more than $1 billion in renewable energy projects in the United States and Europe in recent years, announced in late May its decision to back the Jasper [Solar] Power Project, a 96 MW [megawatt] solar photovoltaic (PV) plant in Northern Cape, with a $12 million investment.

"We only pursue investments that we believe make financial sense," said Rick Needham, Google's director of energy and sustainability. "South Africa's strong resources and supportive policies for renewable energy make it an attractive place to invest."

Abundance of Sun

Once completed, Jasper is expected to be one of the biggest solar installations in the continent, capable of generating enough power for some 30,000 homes.

It's no secret that Africa has plentiful sunshine, with many parts of the continent enjoying daily solar radiation of between 4 kWh [kilowatt-hours] and 6 kWh per square meter. But it's no secret, either, that Africa has the world's lowest electricity access rates, with more than half of its countries experiencing daily—and costly—power outages.

Amid such conditions, experts say investments in large-scale solar power projects could transform a continent faced with fast-rising populations and increasing demand for energy to support its economic growth.

"Six out of the 10 fastest economies in the world (over the past decade) were in Africa, and that requires much more energy, at a faster-growing pace than we've seen before," says Frank Wouters, deputy director-general of the International Renewable Energy Agency.

Ambitious Projects

And some countries have already taken notice. While South Africa is clearly setting the pace, projects are being announced across the continent as more countries look to unlock their massive solar potential.

In late April, Mauritania launched what's described as Africa's biggest solar PV plant so far, a 15 MW facility that is designed to account for 10% of the country's energy capacity, according to its developers. In early May, Morocco began the first phase of the construction of a 160 MW concentrated solar power technology plant near Ouarzazate as part of the country's efforts to produce 2,000 MW of solar energy by 2020.

And late last year, British company Blue Energy announced plans to build the Nzema project in Ghana, a 155 MW facility.

Construction at the $400 million project is expected to begin in the first quarter of next year, while the plant should become fully operational by the end of 2015.

Obstacles

Yet, despite such ambitious schemes, experts say the continent is far from exploiting its massive solar energy potential. According to the International Energy Agency, coal, oil and gas together accounted for 81% of Africa's total power generation in 2009, with nuclear power making up 2%, hydropower 16% and all other renewable sources accounting for just 1%.

Wouters says that a lack of awareness about the current price competitiveness of solar technology, coupled with wider inefficiencies in the performance of most power utilities across the continent, is preventing African countries from scaling up their solar energy production.

Another problem is financing, as higher up-front capital costs, longer payback periods and a lack of solar-project experience in the banking sector make access to funds more challenging.

"You need to involve banks and for many banks in Africa this is also new, so again you have to raise awareness," says Wouters. "Money typically comes with a risk premium which makes it more expensive than necessary."

Actions

Others say, however, that it's inadequate policies and a lack of political commitment that prevent solar from taking off.

"The governments in Africa should change their attitude of thinking that solar is too expensive," says Dickens Kamugisha, chief executive of Uganda-based NGO [nongovernmental organization] Africa Institute for Energy Governance. "Every decision should be based on research that can help in allocating the energy budgets."

Power Africa Initiative to Unlock Investment and Growth

President [Barack] Obama launched Power Africa nearly one year ago to double access to electricity in sub-Saharan Africa—electricity needed for students to succeed, businesses to thrive, and African economies to grow. The challenge is greatest beyond the electric grid serving dense urban populations. More than 240 million people live without electricity in rural and peri-urban communities across the six Power Africa focus countries. Too many do not even show up on government plans to expand the grid over the next decade.

But, bolstered by the falling cost of renewable energy generation; rapid advances in energy storage, smart meter, and mobile payment technologies; and innovative business models, new distributed energy companies are now delivering clean, reliable energy in Africa at a competitive price point. While the market is still young, it holds great promise to follow the mobile phone in leapfrogging centralized infrastructure across Africa.

John Podesta, "Power Africa: Beyond the Grid,"
The White House Blog, *June 3, 2014.*

Last year, a UNEP report said that Africa's power sector needs to install an estimated 7,000 MW of new generation capacity each year. It warned that "unless stronger commitments and effective policy measures are taken to reverse current trends," half the population of sub-Saharan Africa will be without electricity in 2030.

Mark Hankins, director of Kenya-based African Solar Designs, says that in order for Africa to tap its clean energy potential, solar must take center stage in the continent's energy discussions.

"There needs to be a serious reassessment of how to do policy and finance to help solar meet its potential in Africa," says Hankins. "This means not just addressing the needs of poor people—it means using solar to address the energy sector needs for on and off grid and ... using it to help business," he adds. "Solar needs to be at the table, with all of the other technologies."

> "The giant solar thermal array featuring more than 300,000 reflective panels and steam-driven turbine towers has been 'killing and singeing' birds."

Utility-Scale Solar Power Harms Wildlife and Is Not Worth Its Cost

Michael Sandoval

In the following viewpoint, Michael Sandoval reports that at the recently opened Ivanpah utility-scale solar energy plant in California, birds are being killed by the hot air the facility produces. The government's policy, he points out, has been that the benefits of solar power override the environmental impact. However, it is expected that the cost of solar power will remain much higher than that of conventional power sources, and it is uncertain whether government subsidies will continue. In Sandoval's opinion, an expensive technology that has secured its funding through political connections and produced only a small fraction of the nation's power should not be supported by taxpayers' money. Sandoval is an energy policy analyst and investigative reporter at the Independence Institute.

Michael Sandoval, "Fried Birds: Green Energy Involves Tradeoffs Too," Independence Institute, February 17, 2014. Copyright © 2014 by Independence Institute. All rights reserved. Reproduced by permission.

As you read, consider the following questions:

1. According to the viewpoint, how hot does the air get around the turbine towers at the Ivanpah solar plant?

2. According to the Energy Information Administration, in 2018 how much more will it cost to generate power from solar energy than from coal?

3. Why do experts doubt that more solar power plants like Ivanpah will be built in California, according to Sandoval?

The Ivanpah solar plant went online last week [February 2014], but the cost to wildlife—particularly birds—won't be known for at least two more years.

The giant solar thermal array featuring more than 300,000 reflective panels and steam-driven turbine towers has been "killing and singeing" birds by heating the air to around 1,000 degrees Fahrenheit near the towers, according to reports.

All power sources involve trade-offs, but to date, wind and solar have generally avoided discussing the topic, often quickly shifting to pointing out the costs of other energy sources in defending their own environmental impacts.

Policy directives aimed to support the technologies often override such environmental concerns, as they did with Ivanpah [according to a February 2014 article in the *Cape Breton Post*]:

> Ivanpah can be seen as a success story and a cautionary tale, highlighting the inevitable trade-offs between the need for cleaner power and the loss of fragile, open land. The California Energy Commission concluded that while the solar plant would impose "significant impacts on the environment ... the benefits the project would provide override those impacts."

The plant's effects on birds is the subject of a current two-year study.

Causes of Bird Deaths at Solar Energy Plants

Cause of Death	Ivanpah	Genesis	Desert Sunlight	Total
Solar flux	47	0	0	47
Impact trauma	24	6	19	49
Predation trauma	5	2	15	22
Trauma of undetermined cause	14	0	0	14
Electrocution	1	0	0	1
Emaciation	1	0	0	1
Undetermined (remains in poor condition)	46	17	22	85
No evident cause of death	3	6	5	14
Total	141	31	61	233

TAKEN FROM: Rebecca A. Kagan, Tabitha C. Viner, et al., "Avian Mortality at Solar Energy Facilities in Southern California," National Fish and Wildlife Forensics Laboratory, April 2014.

But the cost of electricity from solar sources is and will remain higher than other natural resources, like coal, for the foreseeable future, according to the Energy Information Administration [EIA]:

> The Energy Information Administration says that it will cost new solar thermal plants 161 percent more to generate one megawatt-hour of power than it costs a coal plant to do in 2018—despite the costs of solar power being driven downward.

> On average, conventional coal plants cost $100 to make one megawatt-hour, while solar thermal plants cost $261 for the same amount of power. This data, however, does not take into account the impact of federal, state or local subsidies and mandates on power costs.

Political Connections

The solar thermal installation built by BrightSource Energy received a $1.6 billion loan guarantee from the Department of

Energy in 2011. That loan was secured in no small part due to political connections, according to the Heritage Foundation.

Higher electricity costs as a result of policy directives and crony capitalism, something the Solar Energy Industries Association [SEIA] was readily willing to admit:

> [SEIA president Rhone] Resch said a key issue for the industry will be maintaining government policies that encourage development, including tax credits for solar projects that are set to expire in 2016 and government loan guarantees. "The direct result of these policies is projects like Ivanpah," he said.

Once again, however, the claim that solar energy is a "free" or "no cost" energy source has been upended. Another BrightSource project is receiving similar concerns [according to an article in the *Wall Street Journal*]:

> In response to BrightSource's blueprint for its second big solar farm in Riverside County, near Joshua Tree National Park, biologists working for the U.S. Fish and Wildlife Service told state regulators that they were concerned that heat produced by the project could kill golden eagles and other protected species.

> "We're trying to figure out how big the problem is and what we can do to minimize bird mortalities," said Eric Davis, assistant regional director for migratory birds at the federal agency's Sacramento office. "When you have new technologies, you don't know what the impacts are going to be."

Ivanpah may be the first large utility-scale solar thermal installation in California, and also the last [according to a February 2014 article at Reuters]:

> Though Ivanpah is an engineering marvel, experts doubt more plants like it will be built in California. Other solar technologies are now far cheaper than solar thermal, federal guarantees for renewable energy projects have dried up, and natural gas–fired plants are much cheaper to build. . . .

That means the private sector must fill the gap at a time when building a natural gas–fired power plant costs about $1,000 per megawatt, a fraction of the $5,500 per megawatt that Ivanpah cost.

"Our job was to kick-start the demonstration of these different technologies," Energy Secretary Ernest Moniz said in an interview high up on one of the plant's three towers.

The plant is projected to produce approximately 380 megawatts "during the peak hours of the day," according to BrightSource.

A technology that costs 5.5 times more to build and that delivers electricity that is 161 percent more expensive than coal, and that secures its funding through political connections is not the job of the Department of Energy—or taxpayers' dollars—nor to "kick-start the demonstration of these different technologies."

Not when it produces just 0.24 percent of the electricity in the United States in November 2013, according to the EIA.

Periodical and Internet Sources Bibliography

The following articles have been selected to supplement the diverse views presented in this chapter.

Tina Casey	"Solar Can Provide Grid Reliability—at Less Cost than Gas," CleanTechnica, June 24, 2014.
Mridul Chadha	"South Africa Joins Top 10 Utility-Scale Solar Market List," CleanTechnica, June 30, 2014.
Sudeshna Chowdhury	"Scientists Might Have Figured Out How to Make Solar Power Work at Night," *Christian Science Monitor*, April 16, 2014.
Carole Feldman	"Solar Power in the U.S. Becoming a More Popular, Cost-Saving Option for Homeowners," *Huffington Post*, August 7, 2013.
Denis Hayes and Scot Denman	"As Nuclear Power Dies, Solar Rises," CNN, April 22, 2014.
Brian Milner	"Solar Industry Is Here to Stay—and Grow," *Globe and Mail* (Toronto, Canada), April 3, 2014.
Diana S. Powers	"Solar Power Begins to Shine as Environmental Benefits Pay Off," *New York Times*, November 11, 2013.
Russell Ray	"2014: The Year of Utility-Scale Solar," *Power Engineering*, June 11, 2014.
Cynthia Shahan	"Residential Solar Cheaper than Grid Electricity in 25 States by 2015, Utility CEO States," CleanTechnica, July 1, 2014.
Pete Spotts	"Solar Power Breakthrough Hints at Cheaper Panels for More Roofs," *Christian Science Monitor*, May 5, 2014.

OPPOSING
VIEWPOINTS®
SERIES

CHAPTER 4

What Are the Advantages and Disadvantages of Other Energy Sources?

Chapter Preface

The United States' predominant renewable energy source is hydroelectric power. Referred to simply as hydropower, it represents 7 percent of US power production. In the Pacific Northwest, hydroelectric power provides about two-thirds of total electric power. The state of Washington has so much surplus hydroelectric power that it sells some of it to California.

Hydroelectric power is produced by water flowing through dams that contain generators. It is clean, nonpolluting, and highly reliable. The fuel is free and renewable, and the maintenance costs of a hydroelectric power plant are relatively low. Furthermore, the reservoirs behind dams used for power generation also provide storage for drinking water and lakes for recreation.

So why has the percentage of electricity represented by hydropower been decreasing rather than increasing? Why are there not more hydroelectric plants being built in the United States?

One reason is that most of the major rivers suitable for large dams are already in use. Another is that although hydropower is cheap once the dams and power plants needed to harness the electricity are in place, building them is expensive. Still another major reason is that creating reservoirs behind dams floods land, displacing people who live there and destroying wildlife habitats. Moreover, damming rivers is harmful to fish, and the turbines of a hydroelectric plant can kill fish and underwater plants.

However, there is an even stronger reason why there has been little interest in increasing the percentage of hydroelectric power production. Many states have laws setting renewable power standards—that is, requirements that a specified percentage of power should come from renewable sources by a given date—and some of them do not classify large-scale hydroelectric power as renewable. Advocates of its exclusion say that the purpose of the laws is to encourage the development of new ways to generate power without the use of fossil fuels. However, many people feel it does not make sense to prefer other renewable energy sources over existing ones. "In other words," wrote Jeff Reynolds at the website Freedom-Works, "despite being literally decades ahead of its time, hydro doesn't count because it's already solved the problem before it even existed."

Recently, interest in hydroelectric power has been sparked because older plants are being updated to increase their output. There are a great many existing dams, now used only for flood control, water storage, or recreational facilities, to which generators could be added. This would avoid the problems created by construction of new dams. Although during past decades environmentalists have strongly objected to dams and have even succeeded in getting some removed, many support the increased use of those already in place. "Powering those existing dams is in our view the best way to get new hydro-power capacity," John Seebach of the environmental group American Rivers told the *Huffington Post*. "It's cheaper than building new dams, and it's much less likely to cause additional harm to a river."

Although the authors featured in this chapter discuss the pros and cons of more recently developed renewable power sources, hydroelectric power, in place in the United States for centuries, should not be disregarded as a feasible energy source.

| "Biomass energy plants are highly effi-
cient in harnessing the untapped
sources of energy from biomass resources."

Biomass Energy Is a Prime Replacement for Fossil Fuels

Salman Zafar

In the following viewpoint, Salman Zafar describes the advantages of biomass energy, that is, energy derived from plant materials, animal waste, or other organic material. Zafar claims there are a number of technologies for converting such material into clean energy, thereby reducing the need for waste disposal. Besides lessening greenhouse gas emissions by replacing fossil fuels, Zafar argues that biomass energy is important because it is produced from local resources and thus reduces dependence on foreign imports. Zafar is a renewable energy advisor and chief executive officer of BioEnergy Consult, a consulting and project management company located in India.

Salman Zafar, "An Introduction to Biomass Energy," July 20, 2014 and "Importance of Biomass Energy," April 17, 2014 from BioEnergyConsult.com. Copyright © 2014 by Salman Zafar. All rights reserved. Reproduced by permission.

As you read, consider the following questions:

1. According to the viewpoint, in what two ways does biomass waste-to-energy conversion reduce greenhouse gas emissions?

2. According to some predictions, how much of total world energy may be biomass energy by the year 2050?

3. What is the most common method for producing energy from biomass waste, according to Zafar?

Biomass is the material derived from plants that use sunlight to grow, which include plant and animal material such as wood from forests, material left over from agricultural and forestry processes, and organic industrial, human and animal wastes. Biomass comes from a variety of sources, which include:

- Wood from natural forests and woodlands

- Forestry plantations

- Forestry residues

- Agricultural residues such as straw, stover, cane trash and green agricultural wastes

- Agro-industrial wastes, such as sugarcane bagasse and rice husk

- Animal wastes

- Industrial wastes, such as black liquor from paper manufacturing

- Sewage

- Municipal solid wastes (MSW)

- Food processing wastes

In nature, if biomass is left lying around on the ground it will break down over a long period of time, releasing carbon dioxide and its store of energy slowly. By burning biomass, its store of energy is released quickly and often in a useful way. So converting biomass into useful energy imitates the natural processes but at a faster rate.

Biomass can be transformed into clean energy and/or fuels by a variety of technologies, ranging from conventional combustion process to emerging biofuels technology. Besides recovery of substantial energy, these technologies can lead to a substantial reduction in the overall waste quantities requiring final disposal, which can be better managed for safe disposal in a controlled manner while meeting the pollution control standards.

Biomass waste-to-energy conversion reduces greenhouse gas emissions in two ways. Heat and electrical energy is generated, which reduces the dependence on power plants based on fossil fuels. The greenhouse gas emissions are significantly reduced by preventing methane emissions from landfills. Moreover, biomass energy plants are highly efficient in harnessing the untapped sources of energy from biomass resources.

Worldwide Use of Biomass Energy

Biomass energy has rapidly become a vital part of the global renewable energy mix and accounts for an ever-growing share of electric capacity added worldwide. As per a recent UNEP [United Nations Environment Programme] report, total renewable power capacity worldwide exceeded 1,470 GW [gigawatt] in 2012, up 8.5% from 2011. Renewable energy supplies around one-fifth of the final energy consumption worldwide, counting traditional biomass, large hydropower, and "new" renewables (small hydro, modern biomass, wind, solar, geothermal, and biofuels).

Traditional biomass, primarily for cooking and heating, represents about 13 percent and is growing slowly or even declining in some regions as biomass is used more efficiently or replaced by more modern energy forms. Some of the recent predictions suggest that biomass energy is likely to make up one-third of the total world energy mix by 2050. In fact, biofuel provides around 3% of the world's fuel for transport.

Biomass energy resources are readily available in rural and urban areas of all countries. Biomass-based industries can provide appreciable employment opportunities and promote biomass regrowth through sustainable land management practices. The negative aspects of traditional biomass utilization in developing countries can be mitigated by promotion of modern waste-to-energy technologies, which provide solid, liquid and gaseous fuels as well as electricity. Biomass wastes encompass a wide array of materials derived from agricultural, agro-industrial, and timber residues, as well as municipal and industrial wastes.

The most common technique for producing both heat and electrical energy from biomass wastes is direct combustion. Thermal efficiencies as high as 80–90% can be achieved by advanced gasification technology with greatly reduced atmospheric emissions. Combined heat and power (CHP) systems, ranging from small-scale technology to large grid-connected facilities, provide significantly higher efficiencies than systems that only generate electricity. Biochemical processes, like anaerobic digestion and sanitary landfills, can also produce clean energy in the form of biogas and producer gas, which can be converted to power and heat using a gas engine.

Advantages of Biomass Energy

Bioenergy systems offer significant possibilities for reducing greenhouse gas emissions due to their immense potential to replace fossil fuels in energy production. Biomass reduces emissions and enhances carbon sequestration [removal of carbon from the atmosphere] since short-rotation crops or forests established on abandoned agricultural land accumulate carbon in the soil.

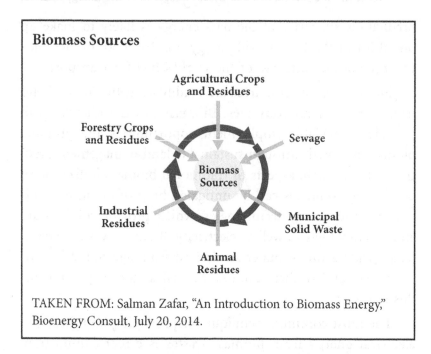

Biomass Sources

Agricultural Crops
and Residues

Forestry Crops
and Residues

Sewage

Biomass
Sources

Industrial
Residues

Municipal
Solid Waste

Animal
Residues

TAKEN FROM: Salman Zafar, "An Introduction to Biomass Energy," Bioenergy Consult, July 20, 2014.

Bioenergy usually provides an irreversible mitigation effect by reducing carbon dioxide at the source, but it may emit more carbon per unit of energy than fossil fuels unless biomass fuels are produced unsustainably. Biomass can play a major role in reducing the reliance on fossil fuels by making use of thermochemical conversion technologies. In addition, the increased utilization of biomass-based fuels will be instrumental in safeguarding the environment, generation of new job opportunities, sustainable development and health improvements in rural areas.

The development of efficient biomass handling technology, improvement of agroforestry systems and establishment of small- and large-scale biomass-based power plants can play a major role in rural development. Biomass energy could also aid in modernizing the agricultural economy.

When compared with wind and solar energy, biomass plants are able to provide crucial, reliable baseload generation. Biomass plants provide fuel diversity, which protects communities from volatile fossil fuels. Since biomass energy uses domestically produced fuels, biomass power greatly reduces our dependence on foreign energy sources and increases national energy security.

A large amount of energy is expended in the cultivation and processing of crops like sugarcane, coconut, and rice which can be met by utilizing energy-rich residues for electricity production. The integration of biomass-fueled gasifiers in coal-fired power stations would be advantageous in terms of improved flexibility in response to fluctuations in biomass availability and lower investment costs. The growth of the bioenergy industry can also be achieved by laying more stress on green power marketing.

"There is no quicker way to move carbon into the atmosphere—the opposite of what we want—than through utility-scale biomass energy plants that burn millions of trees per year."

Biomass Power Plants Produce Just as Much Pollution as Coal-Fired Power Plants

Gordon Clark and Mary Booth

In the following viewpoint, Gordon Clark and Mary Booth point out that although biomass energy has been promoted as environmentally friendly, new and proposed biomass power plants emit just as much pollution and carbon dioxide as those using fossil fuels, sometimes even more. The arguments favoring biomass power plants as a renewable energy source are not valid, they say; recent studies have shown this, and some states are eliminating subsidies and tightening regulations requiring efficiency. The authors speculate whether the Environmental Protection Agency will take federal action and formulate rules that make biomass power plants responsible for the greenhouse gases they release. Booth is the director of the Partnership for Policy Integrity, and Clark is its communications director.

Gordon Clark and Mary Booth, "Dispelling the Myth of Clean, Green Biomass Power," Truthout, March 15, 2013. Copyright © 2013 by Truthout. All rights reserved. Reproduced by permission.

As you read, consider the following questions:

1. According to the viewpoint, what is the main fuel that would be burned by most of the proposed biomass energy plants?

2. According to the authors, what is wrong with the claim that the amount of carbon released from burning biomass materials is no greater than it would be if the materials were left to decompose?

3. According to the viewpoint, how much wood per megawatt is consumed by utility-scale biomass energy plants?

Promoted as clean and climate friendly, and driven by lucrative renewable energy subsidies and tax credits, biomass energy—burning wood and other biological materials to produce heat and power—is on the rise around the United States, with hundreds of new facilities large and small proposed in the past 10 years. However, recent scientific and policy developments recognizing that biomass energy has significant greenhouse gas emissions have blown a major hole in arguments for treating biomass as a favored renewable energy source and could fundamentally reshape its future in the United States.

Until this past decade, the nation's aging biomass fleet was composed largely of industrial boilers, often located at sawmills and paper mills, which burned manufacturing waste or waste wood to produce industrial heat and power. Some of these facilities also exported electricity to the grid. In recent years, however, there has been a surge of over 200 proposals for new biomass power plants in the United States. Eligible for lucrative renewable energy subsidies and tax credits, most of these proposed plants are stand-alone electricity-generating units, uncoupled from a manufacturing facility, that plan to produce "renewable" power for the grid. Critically, most of them plan to burn wood—wood that is directly sourced from logging operations—rather than waste from paper mills and other wood-processing facilities.

Citizens in the communities where these new biomass facilities are proposed often find the plans alarming. A moderate-sized biomass power plant in the 30–40 megawatt (MW) range (they can exceed 100 MW) is a huge installation, with a 200- to 300-foot smokestack, a wood chip pile 60 feet tall that can cover several acres, and an unending stream of tractor-trailers delivering wood fuel. Cooling towers blow off hundreds of thousands of gallons of water a day as waste steam, water that is often taken from nearby rivers.

Also to many local residents' surprise, these biomass power plants emit just as much pollution, and in some cases even more, as coal-fired power plants—tons of particulate matter, carbon monoxide, nitrogen oxides, volatile organic compounds, hydrochloric acid, and carcinogens like formaldehyde and benzene. They also emit carbon dioxide, the primary global warming gas, and lots of it—far more, it turns out, than fossil fuel plants. Burning fuels with low energy density and high water content, biomass power plants are notoriously inefficient and actually emit 40–50% more carbon dioxide per megawatt-hour than coal plants, and more than 300% the carbon dioxide of gas plants.

Flawed Arguments

How did something that emits so much conventional pollution, and more greenhouse gases than coal, come to be incentivized as "green" energy?

To some extent, this has been the fault of policy makers who were eager to advance the cause of renewable energy and failed to critically examine biomass power. They accepted the two main arguments usually advanced for biopower's supposedly benign effect on the climate: first, that the carbon released from burning waste materials such as sawmill trimmings and logging residues (tree tops and branches) is no greater than the carbon released if those materials are left to decompose; and second, that biomass fuels such as switchgrass and trees can be grown and harvested in such a way that each new crop would absorb or "resequester" equivalent carbon as was released by the burning of the previous crop. In either case, there is supposedly no net increase in carbon dioxide emissions—or so the theory goes—and biomass is therefore as "carbon neutral" and "green" in many policy makers' minds as wind or solar.

There is a major and obvious flaw in each of these propositions. The problem with the burning-is-the-same-as-decomposition argument is that burning takes minutes, while decomposition takes years. (Moreover, decomposition of logging residues helps build long-lived soil carbon stocks for healthy forests.) The problem with the "just wait and it will regrow" argument is even more blatant. Switchgrass crops may indeed be regrown swiftly after harvest, but in fact, there are virtually no biomass facilities using switchgrass or other energy crops as fuel, due to prohibitive costs and logistics. Most existing and proposed biomass plants burn wood, but while it takes mere moments to cut and burn a tree, it takes decades to regrow a new one in its place. This fact is widely recognized when we bemoan the role forest loss plays in driving global warming, yet it goes curiously unnoted in the promotion of wood fuels—indeed, the exact opposite is assumed, and burning wood magically becomes "carbon neutral."

Perhaps because of growing public concern over the state of our forests, energy companies and the biomass industry have hastened to portray the newly emerging fleet of biomass plants as using mostly logging residues and other waste wood for fuel, attempting to keep greenhouse gas impacts more squarely in the "it would decompose anyway" zone. However, this argument collapses the moment one reads the permit for one of these plants.

Utility-scale biomass energy plants consume huge amounts of wood—about 12,500 green tons per megawatt per year. The air permit for the 75 MW Laidlaw biomass plant in Berlin, New Hampshire, for instance, states the facility will burn 113 tons of "whole logs" an hour—nearly a million tons a year, or the equivalent of clear-cutting more than an acre of forest every hour. Such prodigious demand far outstrips available logging residues in most regions, meaning that each new facility requires cutting hundreds of thousands, if not millions, of trees each year—trees that would otherwise continue growing and sequestering carbon dioxide out of the atmosphere.

Recent Studies

The good news for the planet is that the renewable energy policies rewarding such polluting, forest-threatening power plants were written a number of years ago, and in the interim, as local activists have fought individual plants, the science of carbon accounting for biomass has taken big leaps forward. The results have not been good for the industry.

Given its extensive forest cover and centuries-old tradition of burning wood, New England has been a hotbed of biomass energy development—as well as citizen opposition to it—so it's not surprising that Massachusetts became the first state to do some actual scientific analysis of the issue. To make sure the state could meet the greenhouse gas reduction goals set in its 2008 Global Warming Solutions Act, Governor Deval Patrick's administration commissioned the well-regarded Manomet Center [for Conservation Sciences] to study the carbon impacts of biomass energy. The primary finding was that when biomass plants burn a combination of logging residues and whole trees, the net emissions of carbon dioxide, the primary global warming gas, exceed emissions from an

© Andy Singer/PoliticalCartoons.com.

equivalent-sized coal-fired plant for more than 45 years, and exceed emissions from an equivalent gas-fired plant for more than 90 years—even when taking forest regrowth into account.

This central finding was reinforced by a similar study conducted in the Southeast, which examined biomass fuel sourced from fast-growing pine plantations and concluded, "the expanded biomass scenario creates a carbon debt that takes 35–50 years to recover."

The findings of both this study and the Manomet study carry extra weight given that each had a coauthor from the Biomass Energy Resource Center, a group dedicated to promoting small-scale biomass energy installations.

The scientific reality revealed by these two studies, and a number of others that have emerged in the past two years, is that when it comes to biomass power's relative contribution to global warming, the treatment of biomass as "carbon neutral" couldn't be further from the truth. Industry claims notwithstanding, there is no quicker way to move carbon into the atmosphere—the opposite of what we want—than through utility-scale biomass energy plants that burn millions of trees per year.

Action by the States

In response to the Manomet study, Massachusetts dramatically reduced its subsidies to biomass power, finalizing the regulations in August 2012. The state's Department of Energy Resources' [DOER's] new policy is the first in the nation to acknowledge that utility-scale biomass plants emit massive amounts of carbon dioxide, and thus should not be subsidized as renewable energy to meet the state's greenhouse gas reduction goals. Recognizing that electricity-only biomass plants are only about 24% efficient, less even than the 33% efficiency of old line coal-fired plants, the new regulations require biomass power plants to be at least 50% efficient before receiving half a renewable energy credit (REC) per megawatt-hour, and 60% efficient to receive a full credit. This standard for the RECs, which are worth millions of dollars to a utility-scale plant, can only be met by smaller facilities that utilize waste heat for thermal energy in addition to generating electricity.

The new Massachusetts regulations had an almost immediate impact on the industry. The Russell Biomass project in Russell, Massachusetts, a 50-megawatt wood-burning power plant under development since 2005, was abruptly cancelled less than two months after the new rules were announced.

The Russell project was Exhibit A for the type of tree-burners designed to produce electricity for the grid, with a section in the plant's air permit stating that it would burn 250,000–350,000 tons of whole tree fuel per year, along with municipal wood fuel, stump grindings, and pallet grindings. "Under the final DOER regulations, the project is not technically and economically viable because of the required 50-percent efficiency, coupled with the new forest biomass fuel supply limitations," said Russell Biomass partner John Bos. "We are unable to modify the plant design as permitted."

The new Massachusetts regulations could provide a template for other states that are serious about reducing emissions from the power sector. High efficiency is one commonsense standard that most people can agree on for renewable energy, and simply requiring that plants meet a stringent efficiency standard in order to qualify for renewable energy credits would do much to reduce the stampede of biomass power development now under way.

Action by the states could also soon be coupled with federal action. At the Environmental Protection Agency [EPA], a panel commissioned by the agency to examine the greenhouse gas impacts of biomass energy has concluded that biomass energy cannot a priori be considered carbon neutral, but depends on a number of factors—including whether forests are used as fuel.

It remains to be seen whether EPA will resist the heavy politicization of this issue and write science-based rules that make biomass power plants responsible for the carbon they emit. The moment is ripe, however, for policy makers—including President [Barack] Obama, who espoused a newly awakened concern over climate change during his second inaugural speech and recent State of the Union [address]—to acknowledge that a renewable energy policy that accelerates forest cutting and CO_2 emissions is worse than no policy at all.

> "Some European countries, especially Germany, have launched projects that combine renewables like solar and wind with hydrogen for energy storage, implying clean, zero-emission, stable power grids."

Hydrogen Energy Storage Can Make Reliance on Renewable Energy Sources Practical

Peter Hoffmann

In the following viewpoint, Peter Hoffmann explains that European countries are far ahead of the United States in developing power systems from renewable energy sources that can store intermittent energy such as wind and solar in the form of hydrogen, thus allowing for continuous power. This, he says, makes the use of renewables much more reliable and less expensive than their critics have estimated. Many such projects are already under way in Europe, and in Hoffmann's opinion the United States and other nations should stop lagging. Hoffmann is the editor and publisher of the Hydrogen and Fuel Cell Letter.

Peter Hoffmann, "The Hydrogen Solution," Project Syndicate, April 3, 2013. Copyright © 2013 by Project Syndicate. All rights reserved. Reproduced by permission.

As you read, consider the following questions:

1. According to researchers, how large an electricity grid could be powered by a combination of renewable energy sources and hydrogen storage by 2030?

2. According to the viewpoint, what would be the function of hydrogen in a power system based on wind and solar energy?

3. According to Hoffmann, where is the world's first renewable energy/hydrogen hybrid power plant that produces both electricity and hydrogen as car fuel?

Around the world, governments and businesses are constantly being called upon to make big investments in solar, wind, and geothermal energy, as well as biofuels. But, in the United States, unlike in Europe and Asia, discussion of hydrogen energy and fuel cells as systemic, game-changing technologies is largely absent. That needs to change: These clean, renewable energy sources promise not only zero-emission baseload power, but also a zero-emission fuel for cars and trucks, the biggest polluters of them all.

By now, many have heard about plans by big carmakers—including Honda, Toyota, and Hyundai—to launch hydrogen fuel cell cars commercially around 2015. Daimler, Ford, and Nissan plan to launch such cars around 2017. Germany plans to build at least 50 hydrogen fueling stations by 2015 as the start of a countrywide network. Japan and Korea have announced similar plans.

But a bigger, largely unreported, message is that some European countries, especially Germany, have launched projects that combine renewables like solar and wind with hydrogen for energy storage, implying clean, zero-emission, stable power grids that require no coal, oil, or nuclear power.

Indeed, the bottom line of a new study by two American researchers, Willett Kempton and Cory Budischak, is that the

How Stored Hydrogen Produces Power

Hydrogen energy storage is based on the chemical conversion of electricity into a new energy carrier, hydrogen, by means of water electrolysis in which water (H_2O) is split by the electric current into its constituent elements, hydrogen (H_2) and oxygen (O). Because of its chemical nature, hydrogen is much easier to store and transport than electricity. To provide electricity back to the grid, the hydrogen can be fed into a fuel cell that uses reverse electrolysis (i.e., hydrogen and oxygen will generate electricity and water), or fed into combustion engines similar to hydrocarbons where the hydrogen gas is burnt.

Now existing only in demonstration projects, hydrogen storage has the potential to catch up quickly with alternative solutions.... Its storing phase is already mature in the chemical and petrochemical industries with three large-scale underground facilities in operation in Texas and in the U.K. [United Kingdom]; this is in addition to its well-known use in compressed tanks.

Benoit Decourt, Romain Debarre, and Olivier Soupa,
"Making the Case for Hydrogen-Based Energy Storage,"
Schlumberger Business Consulting, 2013.

combination of renewables and hydrogen storage could fully power a large electricity grid by 2030 at costs comparable to those today. Kempton and Budischak designed a computer model for wind, solar, and storage to meet demand for one-fifth of the US grid. The results buck "the conventional wisdom that renewable energy is too unreliable and expensive," says Kempton. "For example," according to Budischak, "using hydrogen for storage, we can run an electric system that today would meet a need of 72 gigawatts [GW], 99.9% of the time, using 17 GW of solar, 68 GW of offshore wind, and 115 GW of inland wind."

Their study lends scientific support to several such projects under way in Europe aimed at proving that hydrogen gas, converted from water via electrolysis—think of it as natural gas minus the polluting carbon—and stored, for example, in subterranean salt caverns, can smooth out fluctuations inherent in solar and wind energy. It builds in part on two recent studies at Stanford University and the Carnegie Institution [for Science], which conclude that, as Carnegie atmospheric scientist Ken Caldeira put it, "there is more than enough energy available in winds to power all of civilization."

European Hydrogen Energy Projects

The latest effort, scheduled to get under way outside Brussels this year [2013], is the delightfully named "Don Quichote" project ("Demonstration of New Qualitative Innovative Concept of Hydrogen Out of Wind Turbine Electricity"), designed to highlight utility-scale energy storage and transport, and to provide power for fuel cell forklift trucks. The project's partners are a Belgian grocery chain, the European Commission, and various European organizations and companies. Canada's Hydrogenics is providing the electrolyzer and a fuel cell.

Meanwhile, near Berlin, five companies launched a €10 million ($13 million) pilot project at Berlin's main airport in Schoenefeld in December, expanding and converting an existing hydrogen fueling station to CO_2 neutrality by linking it to a nearby wind farm. Earlier last year, two German utilities, Thüga and E.ON, announced two gas demonstration plants. And the world's first renewable energy/hydrogen hybrid power plant, producing both electricity and hydrogen as car fuel, started production in the fall of 2011.

The previous year, German chancellor Angela Merkel laid the plant's cornerstone herself, sending a strong signal of her seriousness about Germany's shift to clean, renewable energy.

Indeed, the much-noted *Energiewende*, or energy turn-around, that she announced in 2010 is arguably one of the most audacious acts of environmental statesmanship yet.

According to the author and environmentalist Bill Mc-Kibben, Germany is in the international forefront of fighting climate change: "The clear alternative and the best news from 2012 came from Germany, the one big country that's taken climate change seriously. . . . There were days last summer when [Germans] generated more than half the power that they used from solar panels." In fact, hydrogen technology will be an integral part of Germany's evolving renewable/alternative energy-based system.

Germany's move toward renewable energy is likely to have a much broader positive impact. A six-article series, "The German Nuclear Exit," in the *Bulletin of the Atomic Scientists* argues that the move away from nuclear energy is already "yielding measurable economic and environmental benefits."

More broadly, Lutz Mez, a political scientist at Berlin's Free University, argues that the country's shift has "observably decoupled energy supply from economic growth," and that the "evolving *Energiewende*, rather than the nuclear phase-out" implies "continuing reforms of social, economic, technological, and cultural policy in Germany."

What, one wonders, are lagging nations waiting for?

| "Talk of hydrogen powering a substantial proportion of the planet's billion cars (and counting) is driven more by techno-optimism than evidence."

Other Energy Alternatives Will Prove More Feasible than Hydrogen Power

Mark Peplow

In the following viewpoint, Mark Peplow argues that although it was once thought that hydrogen would be a clean, efficient fuel for cars, this is no longer likely to prove feasible. At that time, he says, it was expected that nuclear power could be used to produce hydrogen, which could move vehicles more effectively than batteries. However, nuclear power is not presently favored, and batteries have been improved. Peplow claims that although wind and solar power could be used to produce the hydrogen, they will be better used to power electrical grids for charging batteries. He also maintains that hydrogen-powered cars would not significantly reduce carbon dioxide emissions. Peplow is a journalist and former editor who writes for major science publications.

Reproduced by permission of the Royal Society of Chemistry from Mark Peplow, *Chemistry World*, 2013, 10(4), 43.

As you read, consider the following questions:

1. According to Peplow, why did hydrogen originally appear to be a suitable fuel for cars?

2. What energy source is presently used to produce hydrogen, and what is the main disadvantage, according to Peplow?

3. According to Peplow, how much would carbon emissions be reduced if there were 1.5 million hydrogen-powered vehicles on the road?

A sleek car glides past the undulating hedgerows of a country lane. The only sounds it makes are snatches of Vivaldi from the stereo, and the exhaust pipe emits nothing more noxious than water vapour. As it passes, a cloud of butterflies takes flight into the clean summer air.

Proponents of hydrogen-powered vehicles have long envisioned this as the future of motoring. But today, that dream is almost as distant as ever—and increasingly serves as a distraction in the quest to cut greenhouse gas emissions by replacing petrol [gasoline].

At first glance, hydrogen looks like a suitable alternative. It has a higher energy density (by mass) than petrol, and could be distributed to filling stations through pipelines. And although specially designed internal combustion engines can burn hydrogen directly, hydrogen is even more efficient when it drives a fuel cell to generate electricity.

A decade ago, governments and funding agencies drew up ambitious plans to develop cheaper fuel cells and to enable cars to store practicable quantities of hydrogen. In 2003, President George [W.] Bush committed $720 million to the research effort. But by 2009, it was clear that hydrogen was no quick fix, and US energy secretary Steven Chu diverted much of the funding into battery research. It was the right move.

When the 'hydrogen economy' concept was coined in the early 1970s, advocates such as electrochemist John Bockris expected cheap, plentiful nuclear power to produce hydrogen by electrolysing water. Using hydrogen as an energy carrier in this way made sense at the time—power-line losses made hydrogen a more efficient way to move energy over long distances, and battery technology simply wasn't good enough to propel electric vehicles much faster or further than a milk float.

But nuclear accidents, although extremely rare, have made many governments wary of investing in extra nuclear power stations. And they have also exposed the hidden costs of nuclear power: cleaning up the accidents and dealing with radioactive waste.

So, instead, more than 90% of the world's hydrogen is produced from fossil fuels, through steam reforming of natural gas, for example, which also produces carbon dioxide. That carbon dioxide could be sequestered underground, but it isn't, because carbon capture and storage technology is not sufficiently well developed and the costs are astronomical.

Cleaning Up

Wind or solar power could be used to drive electrolysis plants, but isn't that clean electricity better used to feed today's more efficient power grids, and to charge lithium-ion batteries that far outstrip those available in the 1970s? The fuelling points for battery-powered cars are a relatively simple extension to our existing power grid, and new technology is reducing recharging times.

Hydrogen, in contrast, requires an entirely new supply infrastructure. That's why the only hydrogen car on the road was, until recently, the Honda FCX Clarity; just a few dozen drive around Southern California—the only place in the US with a sufficient network of hydrogen filling stations. In February, Hyundai launched its Tucson ix35 hydrogen fuel cell vehicle, and hopes to make 1,000 of them for the European market. Compare that with the European Commission's hydrogen road map, which forecasts an incredible 1 million hydrogen fuel cell vehicles by 2020.

Storing hydrogen on board a car also requires expensive pressure vessels or cryogenic systems. Chemists and engineers have worked hard to find alternatives, such as adsorbing hydrogen onto porous materials, or using hydrogen-dense molecules to release hydrogen on demand. For example, Matthias Beller at the University of Rostock, Germany, recently unveiled a ruthenium catalyst that can generate hydrogen from methanol at a relatively mild 65–95°C.

But while the ruthenium catalyst is a lovely bit of chemistry, it is not a breakthrough for the hydrogen economy: the reaction releases carbon dioxide, which is much harder to capture from millions of cars than it is at a single power station; the catalyst turnover frequency reached $4700h^{-1}$, many orders of magnitude from practicability; and it relies on ruthenium, global stocks of which are thought to be only about 5,000 tonnes.

In February [2013], the UK [United Kingdom] H_2Mobility partnership issued a report suggesting that 1.5 million hydrogen-powered vehicles could be on the road in the UK by 2030. Yet even this optimistic report noted that the effort would only reduce carbon dioxide emissions by about 3 million tonnes—less than the world currently emits in one hour.

Hydrogen will undoubtedly find transport niches, but talk of hydrogen powering a substantial proportion of the planet's billion cars (and counting) is driven more by techno-optimism than evidence. Faster and more significant impacts would come from improving battery technology, investing in clean electricity sources and developing carbon sequestration. The hydrogen economy is alluring, but it is a distraction from the important task of decarbonising our transport system.

Periodical and Internet Sources Bibliography

The following articles have been selected to supplement the diverse views presented in this chapter.

| Jonathan Benson | "New Fuel Cell Technology Produces Electricity from Biomass and Sunlight," *Natural News*, February 28, 2014. |

| Mark Bittman | "The New Nuclear Craze," *New York Times*, August 23, 2013. |

| Jaclyn Brandt | "Tipping the Scales for Geothermal Energy," *FierceEnergy*, July 1, 2014. |

| Tina Casey | "New Report Finds Thermal Energy Storage Could Add Value to Solar Energy," *CleanTechnica*, June 10, 2014. |

| Nick Cunningham | "Five Crazy New Forms of Energy That Just Might Work," Oilprice.com, June 26, 2014. |

| Pete Danko | "Fuel Cells Power Up: Three Surprising Places Where Hydrogen Energy Is Working," *National Geographic*, April 3, 2014. |

| Richard Ecke | "Geothermal Energy Has Potential," *Great Falls Tribune* (Montana), June 15, 2014. |

| Peter Hannam | "Race Against Time: Scientists Push for Energy Switch," *Sydney Morning Herald* (Australia), November 5, 2013. |

| Hydrogen Fuel News | "Geothermal Energy May Not Be as Expensive as It Seems," June 18, 2014. |

| Jake Richardson | "Renewable Energy Saves Fortune 500 Companies over $1 Billion," *CleanTechnica*, June 30, 2014. |

| Bryan Walsh | "The Challenges of America's Energy Revolution," *Time*, October 7, 2013. |

For Further Discussion

Chapter 1

1. After reading the viewpoints in this chapter, do you believe alternative energy sources are essential for powering the world in the future? Explain your answer, drawing upon at least two viewpoints to support your reasoning.

2. Eric McLamb argues that diverse energy technologies must be developed to replace fossil fuels once they are depleted. Why does the author believe these technologies are so important? Do you agree or disagree with McLamb? Explain your reasoning.

3. Louis Bergeron reports on a study conducted by researchers Mark Z. Jacobson and Mark A. Delucchi. Do you agree with Jacobson and Delucchi that the entire world could be powered by renewable sources by 2050? Explain your reasoning.

Chapter 2

1. The viewpoints in this chapter discuss the advantages and disadvantages of wind power. In your opinion, do the advantages outweigh the disadvantages? Draw upon several viewpoints to support your answer.

2. As Erin Ailworth points out, some environmentalists oppose wind power. What are the reasons behind their opposition? Do you believe this reasoning has merit? Why, or why not?

3. Mike Barnard claims that wind turbines do not reduce property values. Conversely, Carl V. Phillips contends that wind turbines do lower property values. Which author offers a more compelling argument, and why?

Chapter 3

1. The authors in this chapter discuss solar power as an alternative energy source. After reading the viewpoints, do you think utility-scale solar power is a practical energy solution? Draw upon examples from the viewpoints to support your answer.

2. Mark Landsbaum maintains that solar power is uneconomical and harmful to the environment. Based on his argument, do you agree or disagree? Explain your answer.

3. Teo Kermeliotis reports on industrial-scale solar power generation in Africa. Although solar programs are under way in a number of African countries, what are some of the obstacles Kermeliotis mentions? Do some of these obstacles also affect industrial-scale solar power generation in the United States? Explain.

Chapter 4

1. Salman Zafar describes the advantages of biomass energy, while Gordon Clark and Mary Booth make a case against this form of energy. What are the main arguments in each of the viewpoints? With which argument do you agree, and why?

2. Peter Hoffmann argues that European countries are far ahead of the United States in developing power systems from renewable energy sources that can store energy in the form of hydrogen to provide continuous power. Based on Hoffmann's argument, do you think the United States should begin investing heavily in this type of technology? Explain.

Organizations to Contact

The editors have compiled the following list of organizations concerned with the issues debated in this book. The descriptions are derived from materials provided by the organizations. All have publications or information available for interested readers. The list was compiled on the date of publication of the present volume; the information provided here may change. Be aware that many organizations take several weeks or longer to respond to inquiries, so allow as much time as possible.

American Solar Energy Society (ASES)
2525 Arapahoe Avenue, Suite E4-253, Boulder, CO   80302
(303) 443-3130
e-mail: ases@ases.org
website: www.ases.org

The American Solar Energy Society (ASES) is the leading association of solar professionals and advocates in the United States. Since its founding in 1956, the group's mission has been to inspire energy innovation and speed the transition to a sustainable energy economy. ASES consists of regional chapters in forty-one states, student chapters across the country, and nearly a dozen technical divisions made up of academic and engineering members from all disciplines. ASES publishes *Solar Today* magazine, and its website features articles on the latest in solar power initiatives, including "Solar Powered Boat Begins Its Expedition to Study the Gulf Stream" and "IKEA Installs Solar Project on the Rooftop of Its 39th U.S. Store."

American Wind Energy Association (AWEA)
1501 M Street NW, Suite 1000, Washington, DC   20005
(202) 383-2500
e-mail: windmail@awea.org
website: www.awea.org

The American Wind Energy Association (AWEA) is the nation's national trade association for the US wind industry. It represents wind power plant developers, wind turbine manufacturers, utilities, researchers, and others involved in the wind industry. With thousands of members and advocates, AWEA promotes the use of wind energy as a clean source of electricity for consumers around the world. The AWEA website offers an interactive map of the United States that shows wind energy facts and initiatives for each state. The website also offers fact sheets, position papers, brochures, and reports such as "Offshore Wind: America's New Energy Opportunity."

Friends of the Earth

1100 Fifteenth Street NW, 11th floor, Washington, DC   20005
(202) 783-7400 • fax: (202) 783-0444
website: www.foe.org

Friends of the Earth is an international organization representing more than two million environmental activists in seventy-four countries. The group is dedicated to protecting the planet from environmental disaster and preserving biological diversity. Toward this end, it supports energy policies that are environmentally and socially responsible. It publishes the *Friends of the Earth* newsmagazine, and its website offers brochures, fact sheets, and reports, as well as the *Climate & Energy Blog*, which provides links to publications such as "Environmental Impacts of Ethanol and Other Biofuels."

National Biodiesel Board (NBB)

1331 Pennsylvania Avenue NW, Suite 505
Washington, DC   20004
(202) 737-8801
e-mail: info@biodiesel.org
website: www.biodiesel.org

The National Biodiesel Board (NBB) is the trade association representing the biodiesel industry in the United States. It acts as the coordinating body for biodiesel research and development in the United States and promotes biodiesel as an integral component of a national energy policy that increasingly relies on clean, renewable fuels. The NBB website provides a section that answers frequently asked questions regarding biofuels as well as fact sheets, reports, and news releases. NBB publishes the monthly *Biodiesel Bulletin*, featuring articles such as "Washington State Reaches Milestone in Biodiesel Use."

National Renewable Energy Laboratory (NREL)

901 D Street SW, Suite 930, Washington, DC 20024-2157

(202) 488-2200

website: www.nrel.gov

The National Renewable Energy Laboratory (NREL) is a laboratory of the US Department of Energy that is dedicated to renewable energy research, development, and deployment. NREL's mission is to develop renewable energy and energy efficiency technologies and practices, advance related science and engineering, and transfer knowledge and innovations to address the nation's energy and environmental goals. NREL's Technology Deployment section of its website features success stories—such as "Wind Energy Education Project Helps Train Workforce of the Future" and "Grassroots Movement Drives Down Solar Prices 30% in Portland, Oregon"—which highlight its technology acceleration activities.

Nuclear Energy Institute (NEI)

1201 F Street NW, Suite 1100, Washington, DC 20004-1218

(202) 739-8000 • fax: (202) 785-4019

website: www.nei.org

The Nuclear Energy Institute (NEI) is the policy organization of the nuclear energy industry. Its objective is to promote policies that benefit the nuclear energy business. The NEI website's Knowledge Center features nuclear energy facts, statistics, and innovations, as well as policy briefs, white papers, reports, and studies. The Knowledge Center also offers an interactive map highlighting nuclear power plants across the United States and specific fact sheets on nuclear facilities and activities in each state.

Office of Energy Efficiency and Renewable Energy (EERE)
Forrestal Building, 1000 Independence Avenue SW
Washington, DC 20585
website: www.energy.gov/eere

The Office of Energy Efficiency and Renewable Energy (EERE) is an office within the US Department of Energy. EERE is concerned with the research and development of energy efficiency and renewable energy technologies. Many of the major areas EERE focuses on are renewable energy generation through biomass, geothermal, solar, wind, and water technologies; sustainable transportation through bioenergy and hydrogen fuel cells; and the efficiency of homes, buildings, and advanced manufacturing. The EERE website offers videos, news, and fact sheets, as well as a blog with articles such as "Energy 101: Promoting Energy Education in the Nation's Colleges and Universities."

Renewable Fuels Association (RFA)
425 Third Street SW, Suite 1150, Washington, DC 20024
(202) 289-3835
e-mail: info@ethanolrfa.org
website: www.ethanolrfa.org

The Renewable Fuels Association (RFA) consists of professionals who research, produce, and market renewable fuels. RFA promotes federal, state, and local government policies, programs, and initiatives that encourage expanded renewable fuel use; provides accurate and up-to-date information to the media, policy makers, and the general public; and participates in educational activities to increase public awareness regarding renewable fuels. The RFA website features statistics, fact sheets, position papers, and reports such as "What Do Biofuels Displace and Why Does It Matter?" and "Biofuels and Their Byproducts: Global Economic and Environmental Implications."

Union of Concerned Scientists (UCS)
2 Brattle Square, Cambridge, MA 02138
(617) 547-5552 • fax: (617) 864-9405
website: www.ucsusa.org

The Union of Concerned Scientists (UCS) aims to advance responsible public policy in areas where science and technology play important roles. Its programs emphasize transportation reform, safe and renewable energy technologies, and sustainable agriculture. The UCS website features a section on clean energy that discusses the benefits of renewable energy use. It offers reports such as "Ramping Up Renewables: Energy You Can Count On," and articles such as "Smart Energy Solutions: Increase Renewable Energy." In addition, its blog offers posts such as "Cape Wind Gets a Big Boost: Clean Offshore Wind Power on the Way."

United States Department of Energy (DOE)
1000 Independence Avenue SW, Washington, DC 20585
(202) 586-5000
website: www.energy.gov

The United States Department of Energy (DOE) is a cabinet-level department of the federal government whose mission is to ensure America's security and prosperity by addressing its energy, environmental, and nuclear challenges through transformative science and technology solutions. The Energy Sources section of the DOE website highlights renewable energy alternatives such as wind, solar, and hydropower. Articles such as "Top 6 Things You Didn't Know About Solar Energy," "A Renewable Boost for Natural Gas," and "Turbines Off NYC East River Will Provide Power to 9,500 Residents" can be found on the DOE website.

United States Energy Information Administration (EIA)
US Department of Energy, 1000 Independence Avenue SW
Washington, DC 20585
(202) 586-8800
e-mail: infoctr@eia.gov
website: www.eia.gov

The United States Energy Information Administration (EIA) collects, analyzes, and disseminates independent and impartial energy information to promote sound policy making, efficient markets, and public understanding of energy and its interaction with the economy and the environment. The EIA website offers a section on renewable and alternative energy sources that features articles such as "California Continues to Set Daily Records for Utility-Scale Solar Energy." In addition, the section features Energy in Brief articles that answer questions relevant to the public's understanding of energy sources, such as how much US electricity is generated from renewable energy? The EIA also publishes the "Annual Energy Outlook," which focuses on factors that shape the US energy system over the long term.

United States Environmental Protection Agency (EPA)
1200 Pennsylvania Avenue NW, Washington, DC   20460
(202) 272-0167
website: www.epa.gov

The United States Environmental Protection Agency (EPA) is the federal agency in charge of protecting the environment and controlling pollution. The agency works toward these goals by enacting and enforcing regulations, identifying and fining polluters, assisting businesses and local environmental agencies, and cleaning up polluted sites. The EPA website features *Greenversations*, a collection of public blogs covering many different topics. Additionally, the website offers a Clean Energy section that provides a Power Profiler that allows users to enter their zip codes to determine the fuel mix that generates electricity in their regions.

Bibliography of Books

Frances Beinecke   *Clean Energy Common Sense: An American Call to Action on Global Climate Change.* Lanham, MD: Rowman & Littlefield, 2010.

Ted M. Bixby   *Green Energy Alternatives: Energy Efficiency and Renewable Technology.* Seattle, WA: CreateSpace, 2010.

Godfrey Boyle   *Renewable Energy: Power for a Sustainable Future.* 3rd ed. New York: Oxford University Press, 2012.

Robert C. Brown, ed.   *Thermochemical Processing of Biomass: Conversion into Fuels, Chemicals and Power.* Chinchester, West Essex: Wiley, 2011.

Robert C. Brown and Tristan R. Brown   *Why Are We Producing Biofuels?: Shifting to the Ultimate Source of Energy.* Ames, IA: Brownia, 2012.

Robert Bryce   *Gusher of Lies: The Dangerous Delusions of "Energy Independence."* New York: Public Affairs, 2009.

Robert Bryce   *Power Hungry: The Myths of "Green" Energy and the Real Fuels of the Future.* New York: Public Affairs, 2010.

Rebecca L. Busby   *Wind Power: The Industry Grows Up.* Tulsa, OK: PennWell, 2012.

Juan José Gomez Cadenas   *The Nuclear Environmentalist: Is There a Green Road to Nuclear Energy?* New York: Springer, 2012.

Martin Cohen and Andrew McKillop   *The Doomsday Machine: The High Price of Nuclear Energy, the World's Most Dangerous Fuel.* New York: Palgrave Macmillan, 2012.

Stephanie Cooke   *In Mortal Hands: A Cautionary History of the Nuclear Age.* London: Bloomsbury, 2009.

Erik Dahlquist, ed.   *Technologies for Converting Biomass to Useful Energy: Combustion, Gasification, Pyrolysis, Torrefaction and Fermentation.* Boca Raton, FL: CRC Press, 2013.

John R. Fanchi   *Energy in the 21st Century.* 3rd ed. Hackensack, NJ: World Scientific, 2013.

Charles D. Ferguson   *Nuclear Energy: What Everyone Needs to Know.* New York: Oxford University Press, 2011.

Trevor Findlay   *Nuclear Energy and Global Governance: Ensuring Safety, Security and Non-Proliferation.* London: Routledge, 2012.

Don M. Flournoy   *Solar Power Satellites.* New York: Springer, 2012.

Philip G. Gallman   *Green Alternatives and National Energy Strategy: The Facts Behind the Headlines.* Baltimore, MD: Johns Hopkins University Press, 2011.

Thomas Gold — *The Deep Hot Biosphere: The Myth of Fossil Fuels*. New York: Copernicus Books, 2013.

José Goldemberg — *Energy: What Everyone Needs to Know*. New York: Oxford University Press, 2012.

Steve Hallett and John Wright — *Life Without Oil: Why We Must Shift to a New Energy Future*. Amherst, NY: Prometheus, 2011.

Eric Jeffs — *Greener Energy Systems: Energy Production Technologies with Minimal Environmental Impact*. Boca Raton, FL: CRC Press, 2012.

Rody Johnson — *Chasing the Wind: Inside the Alternative Energy Battle*. Knoxville: University of Tennessee Press, 2014.

Bob Johnstone — *Switching to Solar: What We Can Learn from Germany's Success in Harnessing Clean Energy*. Amherst, NY: Prometheus, 2011.

Alireza Khaligh and Omer C. Onar — *Energy Harvesting: Solar, Wind, and Ocean Energy Conversion Systems*. Boca Raton, FL: CRC, 2009.

Maggie Koerth-Baker — *Before the Lights Go Out: Conquering the Energy Crisis Before It Conquers Us*. Hoboken, NJ: Wiley, 2012.

Michael Levi — *The Power Surge: Energy, Opportunity, and the Battle for America's Future*. New York: Oxford University Press, 2013.

Mark Lynas   *Nuclear 2.0: Why a Green Future Needs Nuclear Power.* Cambridge, UK: UIT Cambridge, 2013.

Chris Martenson   *The Crash Course: The Unsustainable Future of Our Economy, Energy, and Environment.* Hoboken, NJ: Wiley, 2011.

Leonardo Maugeri   *Beyond the Age of Oil: The Myths, Realities, and Future of Fossil Fuels and Their Alternatives.* Santa Barbara, CA: Praeger, 2010.

Susan Meredith   *Beyond Light Bulbs: Lighting the Way to Smarter Energy Management.* Austin, TX: Emerald, 2009.

Ron Pernick and Clint Wilder   *Clean Tech Nation: How the U.S. Can Lead in the New Global Economy.* New York: Harper, 2012.

Aldo Vieira da Rosa   *Fundamentals of Renewable Energy Processes.* 3rd ed. Waltham, MA: Academic Press, 2013.

Jeremy Shere   *Renewable: The World-Changing Power of Alternative Energy.* New York: St. Martin's Press, 2013.

Jefferson W. Tester, Elisabeth M. Drake, Michael J. Driscoll, Michael W. Golay, and William A. Peters   *Sustainable Energy: Choosing Among Options.* Cambridge, MA: MIT Press, 2012.

Brian F. Towler   *The Future of Energy.* Waltham, MA: Academic Press, 2014.

Charles Weiss and *Structuring an Energy Technology* William B. *Revolution.* Cambridge, MA: MIT Bonvillian   Press, 2009.

Neville Williams   *Sun Power: How Energy from the Sun Is Changing Lives Around the World, Empowering America, and Saving the Planet.* New York: Forge Books, 2014.

Gary C. Young   *Municipal Solid Waste to Energy Conversion Processes: Economic, Technical, and Renewable Comparisons.* Hoboken, NJ: John Wiley & Sons, 2010.

Index

A

S

ORLAND PARK PUBLIC LIBRARY

ORLAND PARK PUBLIC LIBRARY